GIRL WITH
NO JOB

GIRL WITH
NO JOB

THE CRAZY
BEAUTIFUL LIFE
OF AN INSTAGRAM
THIRST MONSTER

CLAUDIA OSHRY

GALLERY BOOKS

New York   London   Toronto   Sydney   New Delhi

G𝕀

Gallery Books
An Imprint of Simon & Schuster, Inc.
1230 Avenue of the Americas
New York, NY 10020

First Gallery Books hardcover edition January 2021

GALLERY BOOKS and colophon are registered trademarks of
Simon & Schuster, Inc.

For information about special discounts for bulk purchases, please contact Simon &
Schuster Special Sales at 1-866-506-1949 or business@simonandschuster.com.

The Simon & Schuster Speakers Bureau can bring authors to your live event.
For more information or to book an event, contact the Simon & Schuster Speakers
Bureau at 1-866-248-3049 or visit our website at www.simonspeakers.com.

Interior design by Michelle Marchese

Manufactured in the United States of America

10 9 8 7 6 5 4 3 2 1

Library of Congress Cataloging-in-Publication Data

Names: Oshry, Claudia, 1994– author.
Title: Girl with no job / by Claudia Oshry.
Description: First Gallery Books hardcover edition. | New York : Gallery
    Books, 2021. |
Identifiers: LCCN 2020029830 (print) | LCCN 2020029831 (ebook) | ISBN
    9781982142865 (hardcover) | ISBN 9781982142872 (paperback) | ISBN
    9781982142889 (ebook)
Subjects: LCSH: Oshry, Claudia, 1994– | Internet personalities—United
    States—Biography. | Girl with no job (Electronic resource)—Biography. |
    Conduct of life—Humor.
Classification: LCC PN1992.9236.O74 A3 2020 (print) | LCC PN1992.9236.O74
    (ebook) | DDC 792.7/6028092 [B]—dc23
LC record available at https://lccn.loc.gov/2020029830
LC ebook record available at https://lccn.loc.gov/2020029831

ISBN 978-1-9821-4286-5
ISBN 978-1-9821-4288-9 (ebook)

To my family, thanks for dealing with me.
I'd be nothing without you.

In memory of my dad, Michael Oshry.
I love and miss you. I hate you for dying.

Contents

Fantastical Delusions

When I get out of bed in the morning, albeit slowly and regretfully, I get out with one goal. Yup, just one. I prefer not to set unrealistic goals for myself. That one goal is just to make people smile. It sounds incredibly corny and cringey but it's true. Even if it's for one second while their coworker is shaming them on a company-wide email or when their roommate ate the leftovers they were saving *again*. To me, that one smile makes a world of difference. Whether it's from a silly meme that made you laugh for half a second or a sixty-minute podcast that made you forget about the fact that your boss hates you. If, because of me, you forgot about how hard life is, even for a second, then I did my job.

If I've learned anything during my twenty-five long years on this earth, it's that being alive is extremely difficult. I don't like to take myself too seriously. I realize that I am not exactly performing lifesaving work on a daily basis. I am no Dr. Drake Ramoray. But when I lay my head down on my pillow at night, I like to think that I am leaving the world slightly brighter than when the day started. I genuinely want to be a positive force in this sometimes-dark world. Everything I do— from my Instagram (@GirlWithNoJob), to my podcast (*The Morning Toast*), to my comedy—is all about bringing bursts of Taylor Swift–flavored joy into the world. That's what I want for this book, too.

Over the course of the last seven years, Girl With No Job started as an online diary and turned into something I never expected it to be—a career. I like to fancy myself the modern-day Bridget Jones, except I'm chubbier; I drink tequila, not chardonnay; and I would never *ever* be attracted to Colin Firth. So, essentially, I'm nothing like Bridget Jones—we just both had diaries at one point.

Just like Bridget, I find myself prone to self-reflection as well as self-deprecation. This book has given me the opportunity to do both. I gathered my best stories and thought about the tough lessons learned. I found the writing process to be challenging, in the sense that I was forced to look at my life as a whole, not just the highlights. I found myself digging into feelings and experiences I hadn't thought about in years. Memories I had intentionally suppressed were coming back to the surface as I began to dig. I had to take a look at my entire life, which unfortunately includes some embarrassing parts. I pretend like I don't, but I care a lot about what people think of me. Part of me was hesitant to write about certain parts of my life in this book for fear of judgment or ridicule, but I have always been honest and transparent with my followers, and this book is no exception.

From launching my first morning show with Verizon, *The Morning Breath*, at age twenty-two, to an epic cancellation when some old (and extremely stupid) tweets resurfaced, to then creating *The Morning Toast* and subsequently the Toast News Network and launching a successful national comedy tour—this journey has been exciting, challenging, and fulfilling in many ways.

Over the last year, my ass cheeks became one with my couch as I sat for hours contemplating my life experiences and the choices I've made over the years. I must warn you, though. I wrote the entirety of this book while under quarantine during COVID-19, so I apologize in advance if I come off a little cynical. I am merely a victim of circumstance.

Writing a book can really inflate one's ego, as if I needed any help in that department. Picturing the crowds of devoted fans waiting in line to get their hands on the juicy pages of my book has been one of the biggest fantasies of my life. Who knows if that'll actually happen, but a girl can dream. I'm nothing if not delusional.

I guess you could say that delusions of grandeur are my superpower. Delusions that I belong on red carpets among the very people whom I have admired and followed for years. Delusions that I will one day waddle out to a sold-out Madison Square Garden crowd. But you know what? That deluded sense of importance and ability has allowed me to accomplish more and put myself out there in ways I never imagined. So, I encourage everyone to believe in themselves in the delusional way that I do. Put yourself out there in ways you've never imagined. Life is full of highs and earth-shattering lows. It's hard not to get caught up in and torn down by all the negativity. But what if, through your own fantastical delusions, you were able to withstand the negativity and continue to grow, to learn, and to put yourself out there? I think you should all believe in yourselves to the point of taking chances and never accepting a slammed door. You should never be too proud or too dismissive to own up to your mistakes. You'll be better off for it, I assure you. So if that's what you take away from this book, I will consider it a success.

What I also want you to take away from this book is a better understanding of who I really am, because in a lot of ways, I feel very misunderstood. I want the world to get to know me a little bit better and to see the unbelievable stuff that has happened to me that made me into the disgraced queen that I am today. This book is a celebration for my followers *and* for those who may have judged me before getting to know the real me. As much as I pretend those people don't exist, they unfortunately do.

This book is also a celebration of all things pop culture. It's for the Toasters, the Swifties, the Bravoholics, and anyone who understands what it means to be a fan. This book is for any person who understands pop culture, social media, and celebrities and wants to talk about them incessantly. If, like me, you *need* to know what exactly happened in that elevator with Solange and Jay-Z, then this book is for you. This book is for any millennial who understands the desire to lie in bed 24/7 and binge-watch *Friends* but can't do that because it's socially unacceptable. This book is for anyone who can take a joke. So, Kim Jong Un, if you're reading this book, put it down.

- - - - - - - - - - -

When I think about who I was at eighteen years old, when I started my blog and my Instagram account, I hardly feel like the same person. I don't know that girl at all. Sometimes I am even ashamed of her. I have grown and continue to grow every day—and I'm not just talking about the notches on my belt. Girl With No Job put me on a path with constant challenges and opportunities to push myself both professionally and personally. I wouldn't be the person I am now if it weren't for those challenges.

Girl With No Job has been a dream come true, one that I've been preparing for since I was a teenager. As a kid, I always wanted to be popular. I used to spend my nights devouring the high school dynamics of the Upper East Side on *Gossip Girl*, of Orange County on *The OC*, and of West Beverly on *90210*. I idolized people like Regina George and Gretchen Wieners. I spent my days living out those teenage daydreams as I imagined myself the star of my very own show, the Cher Horowitz of my own *Clueless*, the Regina George of my own *Mean Girls*.

I used to crave the level of popularity where people would part like the Red Sea for me. And I used to crave that kind of attention no matter the cost. But I've learned a thing or two since then. I've grown up a lot, due in large part to becoming "famous," whatever that means.

I've often asked myself, more times than I care to admit: Am I famous? What does it even mean to be famous? The thing about fame and celebrity is that it's actually inside our heads. I became famous the day I moved into Manhattan as a fresh-faced thirteen-year-old from Long Island. You see, fame came naturally and early for me. And that's what this book is about. Claudia Oshry's easy road to fame and fortune. Except it wasn't easy at all. Remember the time I got epically cancelled? Remember all the times I stumbled—both literally and figuratively? Yeah, me too.

Growth and evolution have become major themes not only in my life but in my brand. Part of the reason I was hesitant to write a book in general is because I don't want to put something into print that I may not agree with in five years. In fact, I probably wrote many things in this book that are completely contradictory to things I said years ago. And that's okay. At twenty-five years old, I'm allowed to change my mind, to form a different opinion based on new information and life experiences. And you know what? You are, too.

The journey to becoming the woman I am today has taught me so much about what it really means to be a grown-up. As we grow, our opinions and perspectives change. We become smarter, savvier, and more aware of the different experiences of others around us. I think that's called empathy?

I still have a lot of growing up to do, believe me. Growing up in the public eye has been a privilege, but I'd be remiss, devastated, and heartbroken if I didn't acknowledge the disadvantages. I've faced a lot of scrutiny, I've agonized over online trolls and criticism, and most of all, I faced the biggest, most soul-shaking time of my life when I was momentarily cancelled in 2018. But I survived, and I thrived.

How mad can I really be, though? I've hobnobbed with some of Hollywood's finest, walked red carpets, and pushed the bounds of my career in ways that were incredibly fulfilling; I have the love of my life, and I have a supportive family close by every step of the way. My career hasn't been without its heartaches, mistakes, regrets, and embarrassments, but I choose, each and every day, to live with joy and mischief, running headfirst into a fantastical delusion that everything will work itself out in the end. And for the most part, it does.

Maybe a healthy dose of delusion is the key to happiness and success. Or maybe I'm full of shit. Either way, the world can be a scary, ugly place, and if my book can give you a few hours away from that reality, well, then I did my job.

So take your seat. The show is about to begin.

CHAPTER ONE

Born Thirsty

July 10, 1994, was a beautiful Sunday in New York City. On the corner of Seventy-Sixth Street and Park Avenue, in an overpriced private room at Lenox Hill Hospital, a star was born. That star was me. According to my parents, I slid out of my mother's womb like a baby seal and proceeded to cry and throw temper tantrums for the next fourteen years.

Although I wasn't technically the middle child as the third of four sisters, I definitely suffered from a severe case of self-diagnosed middle-child syndrome. I was starving for attention, no matter the occasion. My family was unusual. As kids, my sisters and I genuinely liked each other. We still do. Growing up, my friends *hated* their siblings. They couldn't wait to kick them out of their bedrooms once we got home from school. My sisters and I loved each other because we had to, but we liked each other because we wanted to. The four of us crammed into a twin-sized bed almost every night even though we all had our own beds. We made up dances, did gymnastic routines, and performed them for our friends and family. We were a girl squad before girl squads were even a thing. Unlike other siblings I knew, we *chose* to spend time together, whether that involved watching the WB after dinner or fighting about whether *NSYNC or Backstreet Boys was the superior boy band. After years of research, I can now say with absolute certainty that *NSYNC was the better band. "Dirty Pop" for life. Don't come for me.

Throughout middle school, high school, and college, our dynamics were constantly evolving, but that core love we had for one another never wavered. The untimely death of our dad brought us together in ways I never expected. I sometimes feel guilty about the fact that his death made us even closer than we were before. Like somehow, focusing on the positive outcomes of his passing makes me a sadistic bitch. But the relationship I have with my sisters has carried me through some of the hardest days when dealing with that loss, among all of life's other troubles.

Don't get me wrong; I'm not some kind of loser who only hangs out with their family. I have plenty of close friends from school and work, whom I adore, but there's something about

having sisters that's different from any of my female friendships. There's never a question as to whether one of my sisters
will betray my trust or not look out for my best interest. Caroline Manzo said it best, "blood is thicker than water," and my
relationship with my sisters is a testament to that. Our bond is
tighter and more secure than Kim Zolciak's wig, though that's
not saying much.

But I am lucky because my sisters happen to be the greatest group of people in the world. On the rare occasions when
I make the brave decision to leave my house, they're the only
people I want to hang out with. I think that'd be the case even
if they weren't my sisters. They're just that great. You should all
be very jealous.

Olivia is the oldest, then Jackie, then me, then Margo. We're
close in age, with just six years between Olivia and Margo.
A lot of people wonder how four strong-willed, opinionated
women can work together, hang out together, and not be at
each other's throats. We're all different in ways that complement the others, but our love runs deeper than anything else.
Olivia is strong and protective. She's been our "momager," our
Kris Jenner, since we were kids. She's always been a second
mom to us, taking charge and yelling at kids on the playground
if they even looked at us the wrong way. Jackie is the smart
one. She's the one we all turn to for the world's best advice.
She has this uncanny ability to see every issue and every sit-

uation from all possible perspectives. And she thinks before she speaks, which I could never do. She's very articulate and well-spoken. And Margo is our baby. She's my first call when I need a drink and the person I FaceTime at least fifty times a day. It's been incredible to watch Margo grow up right in front of our eyes. I feel like I'm writing my bat mitzvah speech right now . . . "My sisters mean everything to me, please come up and light candle number three."

If you asked my sisters to describe me, they'd probably say that I'm the wild card. I've always been the loudest and craziest one in the bunch. You never know what I'm going to say next. Some call it annoying; I call it refreshing! That's why it shocked everyone when I was the first one to get married. That doesn't usually happen for the Claudia in the family. It's rare to see the wild card get married before the momager.

What seems to be even more puzzling to people is the fact that Jackie and I work together so closely without ripping each other's heads off. We cohost a daily podcast, *The Morning Toast,* so we're together all the time, both for work and just as sisters. The truth is, I secretly hate Jackie. No, I'm totally kidding. She's literally the greatest. We bring balancing energies and skill sets to the table that have been great for building our business. We would be a ship without a captain if it weren't for Jackie. She's really the brains behind the operation. Jackie and I were able to start this business a few years ago and now we have expanded it so that Olivia and Margo could get involved with their own podcasts. It's like the Kardashians but with college degrees.

In order to preserve the household peace growing up, my mom enforced three simple rules. The first was no sharing clothes without permission. As close as we all were, we had to draw the line somewhere. If you wanted to wear something that didn't belong to you, you had to ask nicely and offer up a barter in return. If you came home with someone else's shirt on, which you didn't get permission to wear, you were fucking dead. It was a very serious rule, and we all upheld it for the most part. The second rule was that there was to be no dating or being interested in the same boy. Later in life, this became slightly difficult to navigate since we were all so close in age, but I am grateful as fuck for this rule, because there is something incestuous about making out with a boy who also made out with your sister. It ain't right.

The third, and most enforced, rule was that we always met at the dinner table at six thirty. It was nonnegotiable. As a teenager with an active social life, I used to find the mandatory meals to be a nuisance. They would interfere with my sleepovers and make-out sessions. As an adult, when I look back on that time in my life, I am certain that my sisters and I are as close as we are *because* we ate dinner together every night. We couldn't watch TV or be on our phones; we had to talk to each other. Family dinners were so ingrained in our DNA. I remember being horrified when having dinner at friends' houses that their parents would let them eat dinner in the living room and watch TV. It was anarchy!

I'm sure you can imagine how difficult it was to get a word in at dinner. It was generally a clusterfuck of a conversation. I quickly had to learn to talk louder and faster than everyone else. I'm well aware that one of my worst qualities is that I talk too much. I talk on top of others, cut them off, and don't let them finish their sentences. I like to attribute that unattractive habit to those wonderful six-thirty dinners. You can blame my parents for that one.

Shortly after I was born, we packed up our New York City apartment and headed for suburbia. Long Island, to be exact. We spent the early chapter of our childhood growing up on the grassy knolls of the South Shore. It was a lovely way to grow up, the idyllic suburban childhood you read about in books and see in movies. On the weekends, if we weren't chowing down at the country club, we were kicking ass on the soccer field. We took soccer very seriously in my house and were all actively involved in the local travel soccer league. Shockingly, so was Ali Lohan, Lindsay's less famous sister. Ali played on a competing team in my division, so the biannual games against her team were some of my favorites. As a young pop culture enthusiast, seeing Dina Lohan cheer on her bowlegged daughter was the highlight of my weekends.

My mom was a determined woman who taught us to speak our minds, to look out for one another, and most important, to never betray one another. Whenever we were all together she'd look around at us and say, "When I'm dead, you'll remember this." It was super morbid but it quickly drilled into us the importance of family. She wanted us to know how lucky we were. I am who I am because of my mother. After my father's death, she raised us completely on her own. She taught us what it meant to be independent women and to never rely on a man for happiness. I know some people see my mom as this controversial figure, but I am incapable of seeing her as anyone other than the person who not only gave me life but also gave me the three most important people in my life, my sisters. She taught me to appreciate and respect them, and for that I am so grateful.

We were all kind of tomboyish as kids. If you know what I currently look like, it may come as a shock to you that I was a very active kid. I played soccer and volleyball and even floor hockey at one point (it was a dark time). We lived on the water and my dad loved to boat and fish. So consequently, we loved to boat and fish. I die a little bit when I look back at photos from our family vacations in Florida. At least once per trip our dad took us to IGFA—the International Game Fish Association—which is basically a museum dedicated to fishing. You would have to tie me up and kidnap me now to get me to a museum while on vacation, but as a kid, I loved it so much. We spent lots of time on the water, fishing, Jet Skiing, and water-skiing. My dad didn't care that he had four daughters. We were going to wake up and fish at six a.m. whether or not we had vaginas.

In addition to being sporty as fuck, I was also an incredibly loud kid. I knew I had a great singing voice at an early age, and I wouldn't rest until every person within a ten-mile radius had heard it. In the car home from school almost every day, I sang "Hopelessly Devoted to You" from the *Grease* soundtrack, much to the dismay and sometimes disgust of my sisters. I would force my friends and family to have talent shows in our living room, in which I was the only contestant and also the MC of the show. Like a desperate Midwesterner in line for *American Idol* auditions, I would do anything to rope adults into listening to me sing. I genuinely thought I was entertaining people, giving them the gift of my talent. I now realize that I was actually annoying the shit out of everyone. My parents begged me to go outside and sing in the backyard, but the living room had better reverb, so I politely refused. When I got an iPod Nano for my eleventh birthday, I was ecstatic. I ripped it open so fast and hugged my mom so hard. She told me to look at the back. I flipped it over and saw it was engraved. It said: "Only if you sing in the backyard."

It wasn't all good, though. I try to forget, but I had a lot of anger issues as a kid. That energy I put into singing, dancing, and playing sports also manifested itself in different ways. I threw temper tantrums a lot. And they were beyond your typical temper tantrums. They were mini psychotic breaks.

I don't know why or how, but more often than not, that anger manifested itself as fits of rage that my family called "the abyss" because I couldn't climb out of them. It's so strange—and lucky—that I ended up turning out fine and not in an institution, because at one point, it was questionable.

I was a problematic kid. I remember being so angry that I felt the blood rushing to my head from clenching my fists so hard. I would scream and say terrible things like, "I hope you die!" I would throw shit at people and kick walls. I tried anything to physically manifest my anger. At first, my parents attempted to discipline me using five-minute time-outs. I would scream bloody murder until they let me out of my bedroom. They'd usually let me out after three minutes just so I would shut the fuck up. But even once I was freed, I wouldn't move. They'd open the door and instead of leaving, I would just keep screaming, "LET ME OUT!!" even though it was over. I was clearly a lunatic.

The older I got, the worse the outbursts got. My parents were desperate. They were growing tired of me ruining meals and vacations. My sisters were over my bullshit as well. I lacked enough self-awareness at the time to stop. I couldn't care about anything other than the fact that I was angry.

I knew that I was really out of control when my favorite babysitter, Charlene, didn't show up for work one day. Or the next day either. I was nine years old at the time and it was my first experience with heartbreak. Charlene and I had a really special bond. I loved her so much. Nobody knew where she'd gone. She was there one day and then gone the next. A few days later my parents finally got in contact with her. She said she had moved back to Trinidad. We were so confused but had no choice but to move on. We found out a few weeks later that Charlene hadn't moved to Trinidad. In fact, she was working for another family in the neighborhood who belonged to our country club. Charlene had, allegedly, grown tired of my bullshit and decided she no longer wanted to be our babysitter.

It's probably not surprising to hear that not long after Charlene left, I was taken to see a licensed professional. It was time to get me checked out, and possibly locked up. The therapist said I had a disorder called ODD, or oppositional defiant disorder, which is marked by defiant and disobedient behavior to authority figures. There was some talk about medicating me, but my parents weren't on board and I never saw the therapist again. I wonder how different my life would've been if they had decided to put me on Ritalin. I'd probably be skinnier, that's for damn sure.

I had a perfectly charmed life, so I don't know what the hell I was so angry about. I was triggered by anything—not getting my way, being hungry, being tired, you name it. I feel really guilty about that time in my life and the stress I put everyone under. I was a piece of work and definitely didn't help my parents' already strained marriage. It freaks me out to think that that little nut job was me.

Enter: The Big D. Divorce.

I knew something was up when my mom drove us to Starbucks and let us order whatever we wanted. She was a bit of a health nut, so this was a rarity. She sat us down and let us know that she and my dad were going to be getting a divorce. My younger sister, Margo, had a visible breakdown. She burst into tears and ran out to the parking lot. I just shrugged it off. I was too excited about my Vanilla Bean Frappuccino to care. I don't remember feeling like it was such a big deal. I was definitely shocked, because I didn't feel like there was anything wrong with my parents' marriage, but I wasn't devastated over it. I had seen tons of movies and TV shows where people got divorced and it didn't seem like such a life-altering event. Hallie Parker and Annie James lived fabulous lives as children of divorce in *The Parent Trap*. Why couldn't I? Plus, my mom also dropped the bomb that we'd be moving back into the city post-divorce, and that, plus the Vanilla Bean Frappuccino, was enough to satiate me.

After the divorce papers were filed, we packed up our house and headed back to Manhattan. Our dad stayed in Long Island. It sounds like a traumatic transition, going through a divorce and having to move, but I loved every minute of it. Granted, our apartment in Manhattan was smaller than the digs I was used to, but that apartment became my favorite place in the world. It still is. Living in the city was a dream. I felt like Carrie Bradshaw (until I grew up and realized that she was the most self-involved narcissist in the history of TV).

My issues with anger eventually mellowed out, right around the time of my parents' divorce. You'd think that having to move schools and deal with a divorce would send me into a tailspin of rage, but it didn't. I started the eighth grade at a new school in Manhattan and I don't remember having many tantrums after that. I sensed there were enough problems in our family. I didn't need to start up with my bullshit now. I wanted to make life easier for my mom because I knew she was struggling. I didn't want to contribute to that. She was responsible for all of us now. We were on our own, without our dad at home. Who wouldn't be freaked out?

Our new post-divorce life consisted of living and going to school in the city and seeing my dad on the weekends in Long Island. It was a pretty standard child-of-divorce life, and I don't remember disliking it. I was (and continue to be) so pretentious that I remember liking the idea of having a "weekend house." It sounds shallow, because it is, but maybe that's just how I coped with it. I didn't feel deprived. My dad came into the city a lot for dinner and my parents still worked together to parent us. We had this exciting new life in the city, which distracted me from realizing that I was sad about the divorce. My parents rarely fought in front of us, and while it wasn't easy for them, they did a good job of keeping us out of it. I'm really grateful for that. And I'm grateful for the life that I ended up having in the city. So much of who I am can be attributed to spending my formative years in Manhattan. I don't have a lot of resentment about the move or the divorce. I really understood that they weren't happy together.

I adjusted well that first year in Manhattan. I made lots of friends, most of whom I'm still close with to this day. I started high school in the fall of 2008, and I was really excited about it. I was thrilled to be at a bigger school with older kids, specifically boys. Eighth grade had gone well for me, so I was ready to strut down the halls of Ramaz Upper School with my LeSportsac backpack in tow. I had a fabulous group of friends whom I loved and trusted like sisters. Assuming high school was going to be something like what I saw in the movies, I was preparing myself for four years of keg stands and house parties. Olivia and Jackie were both in high school at the same time as me. I was a freshman, Jackie was a junior, and Olivia was a senior, so that *should've* been really fun. But a month into my freshman year of high school, in October 2008, BAM! My dad decided to drop dead. Very, very uncool of him.

I was genuinely shocked. As in, surprised. He was only fifty-two years old and in relatively good health for a chubby Jew who loved cigars. We had just had dinner with him not two days before. I wasn't sure how someone could be alive one day and then dead the next. It made no sense to me at the time. It still doesn't. But life has a way of ripping the rug right out from under you when you least expect it.

I'll never forget how we found out that he had died, because it was all so unassuming. It was a Saturday morning and my sisters and I were doing what we did every Saturday—nothing. We were all in the living room watching *Bratz: The Movie* when the phone rang. Nobody flinched or moved to pick it up because that wasn't our job. My mom got off the phone, came into the living room, and told us to pause the movie. She leaned up against the wall and started crying. It's weird to see your parents cry. She said, "I really don't know what to say. Your father died. He had a heart attack. Get in the car."

We were all freaking out, screaming, crying, and so confused. Whoever had called my mom was still at the hospital. My mom had said, "Don't touch him. We're coming." We all threw on our Ugg boots in a frenzy and headed for the elevator.

We made our way downstairs to the parking garage. As we crossed the street, sobbing, I distinctly remember an elderly woman staring at us like we had some sort of infectious disease. My mom whispered, "Their father just died." I'm not sure what we expected this random stranger on the street to say but I looked up at her, hoping to hear some elderly wisdom. She said, "Oh, well. It happens!"

We got in the car and I remember driving over the Fifty-Ninth Street Bridge, sitting behind the driver's seat and thinking: *This is fucking bullshit*. It's that state of shock where you just can't believe that someone's dead. He wasn't sick, he didn't have cancer. He just died on a random Saturday, out of nowhere. He had just come back from the gym and wasn't feeling well. He decided to lie down and subsequently dropped dead while taking a nap.

When we got to South Nassau hospital, we walked into room number 31 and saw him lying there, dead as fuck. They had used a defibrillator on him, so his shirt was ripped open. It was one of his favorite shirts. He always dressed like he was going fishing. Regardless of the weather, Michael Oshry could be seen sporting a fishing shirt, cargo shorts, and boating shoes. He looked like the Jewish Luke Combs.

It was the first time I had ever seen a dead body. The four of us just stood there by his side. We said nothing, just looked down at the shell of a man who used to be our dad. I was afraid to touch him; his body was still warm. It was hard to believe he was actually dead. I wanted to slap him and tell him to wake the fuck up, but I refrained. I didn't want to leave the room because I knew once I left, it would be over. He would really be dead.

We stayed at the hospital for a while and then drove back into the city. It was a forty-five-minute drive filled with nothing but silence. Nobody knew what to say. When we got back into the city, someone (probably me) suggested food. So, we did what we do best—eat pizza.

In Judaism, it's mandatory that you bury the body of a dead person within a day after they die, so the funeral was arranged very quickly. It was held near our house in Long Island. We had only been at our new school for a year at that point, so not many people knew our family yet and even fewer knew my dad, who lived on Long Island. I remember standing outside of the funeral home, greeting everyone as they came in, when three huge school buses pulled up. One of our classmates, Ethan Stein, had organized our entire high school to show up and pay their respects. It was kind of incredible, seeing all these people show up for us when they barely knew us. I had felt so isolated and alone when my dad passed away that seeing my classmates made me feel so seen. It meant a great deal to me and still does. To this day, I cry every time I think about it. I'm crying right now.

All four of us spoke at the funeral. I really didn't want to speak but all my sisters were, so I wasn't going to be the only asshole who didn't. It was awful. I hate crying to the point where I can't talk. I hate watching other people cry; it makes me so uncomfortable. I didn't want my friends in the audience to feel weird seeing me cry. But I knew I'd always regret it if I was the only daughter who didn't speak at my father's funeral. I wasn't old enough or mature enough to really process what I was feeling. My speech was weird and full of metaphors about roller coasters. Don't ask.

I got so many lovely messages and texts during that awful period in my life, and as shallow as it may sound, it felt really good to know that so many people were thinking of me. I've always craved other people's attention, and mourning my father's death was no exception. One of my classmates, Deborah, was on the floor hockey team with me. She was such a nice girl, although we weren't really that close. She wanted to become a rabbi, and I wanted to become a pop star, so suffice it to say we didn't have much in common. Shortly after the funeral, she wrote me the loveliest Facebook message, which I've never forgotten. My dad loved (and couldn't believe) that I was on the floor hockey team and he had come out to watch a few games, cheering me on loudly from the stands. It was just so nice of Deborah to reach out, and I remember being really struck by her message. She wrote:

> I really just want to let you know how sorry I am for your loss of your father. I remember seeing him at all of our hockey games, and he was just truly a great father.

It was such a nice (and random) thing for her to remember. I felt so seen, like she remembered him just as I did in that moment. So now, when someone I know is dealing with grief, I always make it a point to send flowers or a really genuine, long text recalling a specific moment or characteristic. I don't care if they don't respond or say thank you, I just want them to feel how Deborah made me feel.

Grief is weird, because it's absolutely awful but in a lot of ways it changes you for the better. For me, I feel like it made me a more empathetic person. I saw the world completely differently. I'd always been kind of a bitch, but losing my dad opened my eyes to the fact that everyone has their own shit going on.

Grief has also taught me to try to look at every situation life throws at you in a positive light. Which, as a natural born pessimist, can be challenging. When I look at the death of my father, I always think about how lucky I was to have so many people around me. Not everyone is as lucky. If my dad hadn't passed away, I don't think I ever would have met my husband, Ben, because it made me more open to accepting people into my life and not being so rough around the edges. It put me in a different place in my life.

My sisters and I really leaned on each other as we tried to move forward. We took it one day at a time because that was literally all we could do. If one of us couldn't get through the day without crying in the bathroom, then we all cried in the bathroom together. People always ask how my sisters and I got through our father's death at such young ages, and the thing is, you have no choice but to get through it. Life goes on without your dad. And you learn that in a very sad, real way. People attend the funeral, sit shiva, pay their respects, check in on you, but eventually, everyone goes on with their life. It's fucking depressing.

The Oshry girls were there for each other more than ever, and we all kept a close eye on Margo, who definitely struggled with the loss more than any of us. She's the youngest, and she hadn't had her bat mitzvah yet, which, as a burgeoning Jewish woman, is the pinnacle of adolescence. Having a dad was an integral part of all of that. She felt robbed because we all got to have our dad at our bat mitzvahs. We all celebrated becoming women when our parents were still married. Our bat mitzvahs were lavish events thrown at our country club in Long Island, a Jewish girl's dream! Margo didn't get that. She didn't get two parents who were married, and worse yet, she didn't even get a dad. She got to spend the least amount of time with him. She still takes it the hardest. On Father's Day and his birthday, she's the one who needs to be looked after the most. Seeing any of my sisters cry always makes me cry. Especially Margo.

But, rest assured, Margo's bat mitzvah was quite an event. We rented out the flagship Dylan's Candy Bar and it was fabulous. We all overcompensated for what we knew she was missing that day. We danced harder than we had at any of our own parties. She had an ice-cream bar, a candy bar, custom gift bags, and, of course, enormous blown-up photos of herself from a colorful photo shoot we'd set up in our living room a few months prior. Side note: She kept those photos hanging in her bedroom till she turned twenty-one. I like to think that she looks back on that night fondly. It was the first time since my dad had died that I remembered what it was like to be happy.

I've continued on through life missing my dad but never letting grief ruin my life. I dealt with grief in a rational way. I cried when I was sad and I didn't when I wasn't. There would be multiple days at a time where I would completely forget about my father's death. Upon remembering that my father had, in fact, died, I would feel this huge wave of guilt wash over me for ever having forgotten that my dad was dead. It's a difficult balance to uphold, but after a while you just get used to it.

There were a good five or six years where I felt at peace with the loss of my father, but the older I got, the more challenging it became for me not to have a dad. There were more major life moments happening, and the absence of my father was felt more than ever before. I got to see all my friends dance with their fathers at their weddings, but when I got married, at twenty-three, that didn't happen for me. Every girl wants to dance with her dad on her wedding day and have him walk her down the aisle. Watching all of my sisters walk down the aisle without our dad really pissed me off. Watching my sister Olivia give birth for the first time, knowing that her daughter wouldn't have my dad as her grandfather, made me really sad.

Getting married as a child of divorce is weird, but it's also exciting because you feel like you can do it better than your parents did. I got really lucky with Ben. He is there for me more than anyone else. He encourages me to lean on him when it comes to talking about my dad and grieving properly. From the moment we met, Ben wanted me to know that I could feel safe opening up to him. Sometimes I think he's shocked at how little I want to talk about it though. And it's not because I'm in denial, nor am I bottling up my emotions. I just choose not to live in grief. I hate being sad. I want to be happy. It doesn't diminish how much I love and miss my dad if I don't cry every day. Of course, my father's absence hits me every now and then because it's a natural part of the grieving process. But I refuse to spend my life being sad.

Grief is something I'll always live with but won't focus on. I choose to be grateful for what I have instead of focus on what I don't have. To say I was deprived of anything as a child would be hypocritical. I had, and still have, a very privileged life. I choose to be happy and not wallow in sadness. I acknowledge my feelings but I've moved on with my life. It may sound callous but it's not; it's survival.

Very few people are willing to talk openly about their grief. Sometimes I'd like to be able to bring my dad up in a conversation casually and share a story of something he would do or say, but I am aware that it may make people uncomfortable. So I don't say anything, which sucks. I want to help normalize the fact that many of us experience death and loss and learn to live with grief. It's okay to be open and vulnerable sometimes, but it's also okay to want to have fun and focus on what you do have. I want to remember my dad with a cigar in his right hand and a Grey Goose on the rocks in his left. I even want to remember his awful the Mamas and the Papas CD collection.

My dad never got to see me sell out the Beacon Theatre. He never got to see me perform stand-up. He never got to see me release this (hopefully bestselling) book. That's something that I live with every day. But I am reminded every time I smell a cigar that he is looking down on me, beaming with pride (or shame, depending on what day it is).

After my father's death I remember, so badly, wanting life to go back to normal in all the ways that it could. I was eager to go back to school and throw myself back into my friends, my school-work, sports. I didn't want the negative attention at school, I just wanted my life back. I knew kids growing up who had lost parents and that was always their *thing*. They were the kid with the dead parent. I refused to accept that as my fate. I did everything I could to be the funny girl, the girl with a good voice, the girl you wanted to be around. I was trying so hard to make people think of me differently that I think, in the end, they just thought of me as annoying. But I'm okay with that.

When I returned to school, I was ready to dive into what I thought the life of a high school student should be. All the movies I was obsessed with—*Clueless, Mean Girls,* and *Bring It On*—ingrained in me how iconic high school is supposed to be. I wanted to be head cheerleader and I wanted to date the quarterback. But my Orthodox Jewish high school had neither a cheerleading squad nor a football team. I still made the best of those four years.

You would think my love of performing and captivating audiences would be persuasive, but I made the decision early on not to get into musical theater during high school. Even though I knew I could sing better than half those snot-nosed kids, I didn't want to be associated with the stigma of being a "drama kid." Which is ironic because, if you think about it, that's exactly who I was—a dramatic kid. But I had seen *Mean Girls* one too many times and thought that I couldn't be popular while also following my passion for singing. As I'd learned from the fictional halls of the Constance Billard School for Girls and North Shore High, you couldn't be a drama geek and a popular kid. It was an antiquated view of high school but it was what I genuinely believed. I cared more about being well-liked than anything else. At one point I did join the choir for half a second, but I dropped out immediately because it was so lame. Plus, I really struggled to be a part of an ensemble in choir. I was a soloist through and through, so when I didn't get the first solo, I bailed.

A part of me likes to think that I succeeded in becoming well-liked in high school. When I look back at that time, through my rose-colored glasses, I like to think I achieved the Regina George level of popularity, but I am now self-aware enough to realize my peers most definitely found me annoying. I should've known I wasn't as popular as I thought I was when I ran for student council and lost. I had hoped to win the coveted position of senior vice president and even came up with a genius *Jersey Shore*–themed ad campaign based on the promise of GTL: gym, Torah, and learning.

I was horrified and genuinely shocked when I didn't win, seeing as how it was clearly a popularity contest. I brushed it off like it wasn't a big deal even though I was screaming on the inside. I should've known then I wasn't half as cool as I thought I was, and maybe I should've just rejoined the damn choir.

If I could tell my younger self anything, it would be to listen to who you really are and run with it. I would also tell her to start getting her upper lip waxed ASAP. I wonder if I would have found so much joy and fulfillment in following my passions for drama and singing. What if I hadn't let my superficial desire for popularity get in the way of my talent? I could have very well been the next Barbra Streisand, a fabulous actress with a killer voice and a bold sense of self. Imagine if kids everywhere stopped bending to the peer pressure of high school and pop culture tropes and just started living their lives.

Or maybe that's all bullshit, and the real lesson here is that some people were just born to shine and nothing—not even crippling teenage self-doubt, loss, or grief—can get in the way of that.

CHAPTER TWO

A Career Is Born

I grew up in Manhattan, and like any self-involved teenager in New York City, I spent my days hanging out with my friends, thinking we were cooler than we actually were, and, of course, eating my way through the Upper East Side in a knee-length skirt. As a young pop culture enthusiast, I fancied myself the chubby, Jewish Blair Waldorf, replete with the headband and affinity for alcohol. In reality, I was more of a Dorota than a Blair, but I refused to think of myself as anything other than a Queen Bee.

I went to a small Jewish high school in the city, where my peers and I reluctantly studied the Torah and the Talmud every day, along with standard secular subjects. Sandwiched between algebra and American history were in-depth discussions as to why the Jews wandered the desert for forty years. After studying Jewish history from grades K through twelve, I still don't really understand why God made us wander for forty fucking years. What I do know is that I am grateful I wasn't born in biblical times. I do not have the stamina for that kind of cardio. But I loved every minute of high school. I mean, I hated studying and writing papers. I wasn't good at any of it, but I loved my friends and even some of my teachers, if you can believe it.

I was the only one of my friends who had a TV in their bedroom, which meant I spent every night imagining myself walking down the halls of the high schools featured on my favorite shows—*Gossip Girl*, *The OC*, and *Pretty Little Liars*. I wanted so badly to be friends with Serena van der Woodsen and Aria Montgomery. I wanted to be just like them. At one point, I even tried to start a love affair with my English teacher, in the hopes that it would be something like Aria and Ezra from *Pretty Little Liars*. But that's a story for another chapter.

- - - - - - - - - - -

As my senior year approached, I knew it was all coming to an end. All the movies and TV shows I worshipped had prepared me for how sad graduation would be. It would be the end of an era. I would soon have to trade in my Hebrew letters for sorority letters, and I wasn't looking forward to it as much as my classmates were. It seemed so unfair. I was peaking. Life was *just* getting good; why did it all have to change? Boys were finally talking to me! They were also making out with me. I had worked tirelessly throughout high school to find my place as the cute, funny girl, and by my senior year I had finally done it. I had tons of friends, had a phenomenal fake ID courtesy of a classmate's cousin who worked at the DMV, and was invited to almost every party. In a few months, we'd all be going our separate ways for college, and my carefully cultivated social status was going to be worth nothing. It didn't make sense.

I didn't really have big dreams when it came to college. To be honest, I didn't understand all the college hype. Some of my friends fell in love with certain schools or cities. They couldn't wait to spend the next four years repping their school colors at tailgates and vomiting at seven in the morning. But for me, I loved high school so much that I never wanted it to end. I applied early admission to NYU as a physics major. The only A I'd ever gotten in high school was in my eleventh-grade physics class, so I figured I might have a future as the next Elon Musk, but without the receding hairline.

I chose NYU not because I dreamed of being an NYU Violet or because I fantasized about wearing a beret around Washington Square Park, but because NYU was safe. It felt like an extension of high school. I didn't want my life to change, and at NYU, it didn't have to. I was going to school in the same city, with a lot of the same people, just fifty blocks downtown.

I didn't make a lot of friends in college. Before you start feeling sorry for me, know it was a *choice*. I chose not to make new friends. I assumed all the students there were weird and artsy, so I made absolutely no effort to fit in because that was never going to happen. Actually, that's not true. At one point during my freshman year, I did buy a skateboard in an attempt to at least look the part of an NYU student. I asked a redheaded boy in my class to teach me how to ride it, in exchange for two slices of pizza on Mac-Dougal Street afterward. After a few lessons on Minetta Street, I decided I was ready for the open roads. I rode that sweet, hot-pink skateboard to my math lecture, but after a block I completely lost my balance and ate shit in front of ten of my classmates. I was splayed out on the concrete, looking like a total moron. I was fine physically but horrified when everyone surrounded me and offered to help me up. That was the first and last time I tried to fit in.

My freshman-year roommate was assigned randomly, and to be frank, it wasn't a match. We were never going to get along. She was a lovely, quiet girl from Cincinnati. We couldn't have had less in common. I wasn't lovely, I wasn't quiet, and I wasn't from the Midwest. Within a few minutes of our meeting, she let me know she had been accepted into many Ivy League schools and had gotten a full scholarship to NYU. She was smart. Like, really smart. She would correct me all the time, even when I wasn't speaking to her. But my real gripe with her, as a roommate and a human being, was the Bath & Body Works body spray she doused herself in every morning. The putrid scent of Juniper Breeze woke me up promptly every morning at seven, when my first lecture usually didn't start till noon. I haven't spoken to her since the day I moved out of the dorm. I wonder what she's up to. I wonder if she ever thinks of me. I wonder if she's writing about me in *her* book.

My group of friends consisted of the same people from high school who also ended up at NYU: Jason, Alicia, Rachel, and Margaret. With a built-in circle of friends who already knew my penchant for binge-drinking Diet Coke and binge-watching *Friends*, I wasn't entirely unhappy with my situation. Plus my sister Olivia was a senior at NYU, which made things really easy for me. Her friends became my friends. It was comfortable and I liked it. People tend to think of me as an extrovert, probably because I am loud and chubby, but secretly, I find most social interactions with new people to be incredibly painful. Trying to make new friends as an adult is one of those interactions I generally steer clear of. I was not up for putting myself out there, so I didn't. I had a few close friends and that was more than enough for me. I've never been the type of girl with a million best friends. Those girls are the worst.

I was excited to be living on my own and do the one thing I could never do at home—get drunk. NYU wasn't exactly the college of my dreams, but it allowed me to spend my weekends doing what I had always wanted to do—go clubbing. If *Gossip Girl* taught me anything, it was that the key to a successful social life is being able to get into a New York City club at any age. I hit the underage club scene, with my fake ID in hand, and never turned back. Actually, I did turn back once when my otherwise stellar fake ID was confiscated at the door of Hotel Chantelle. That was devastating, but thankfully Olivia turned twenty-one the following month and was gracious enough to donate her old learner's permit to her underage sister.

The other major change in my life during my freshman year at NYU was my schedule. My high school was tough. It was a dual-curriculum Jewish day school where we were held hostage from eight a.m. to five p.m., plus extracurricular activities. Looking back, I can't believe I used to wake up so early and do so much every day. I am amazed at the stamina of my teenage self. These days, I can barely get up for my nine a.m. alarm and I am usually back in bed by three p.m.

As a college freshman with sometimes just one class a day, it was a huge adjustment for me. At first, I loved the freedom I had on weekdays. I slept all day and watched *Breaking Amish* all night. I was one of the few students in my dorm who had a TV and basic cable, which made me very popular. That TV saved my life in a lot of ways. I went to bed every night watching *Friends*, which is where my love affair with the series began. My dorm was the place to be whenever an episode of *Real Housewives* was airing. My TV made me cool, and it kept me relevant. I loved that thirty-two-inch Samsung. I owe her a lot.

With so much free time, I had no choice but to eat everything in sight. One of the perks of living on campus was Space Market, the bodega next to my dorm. They had the most amazing double-chocolate-chip muffins. They could be found, wrapped in Saran wrap, right by the register. They were moist on the inside and crunchy on the outside. I was eating at least two muffins a day, sometimes three. I had purchased an incredibly cute Hello Kitty mini fridge for my dorm room, intended to hold water bottles and sodas, but by second semester, that fridge was overflowing with the finest snacks Space Market had to offer. I started to gain weight, slowly and steadily, but I was really happy and never bothered to notice.

Life on campus was pretty great that first semester. I was living my version of a college fantasy—an extended version of high school. I had a few really great friends. My dorm was properly decorated with Taylor Swift and One Direction posters. My fake ID was working well at most places around campus. Oh, and I somehow stumbled onto an iconic episode of television that would later end up on Netflix.

On my way to my least favorite class, Writing the Essay, I decided to cut through Washington Square Park in the hopes of either seeing someone I knew or getting a hot pretzel. Upon entering the park, I was ambushed by none other than Billy Eichner and a huge camera crew for *Billy on the Street*. I didn't care what they were doing, I was just excited to be on camera!

They were filming a segment called "Amateur Speed Sketching," where a contestant, in this case named Barry, was given sixty seconds to draw a photo of a celebrity and then see if random strangers could guess which celebrity he'd drawn. The stranger who guessed correctly would win $25. Billy, Barry, and the camera crew ran up to me and gave me five seconds to guess who was in the sketch. I was under so much pressure and couldn't believe that I'd gotten caught on camera without bronzer, so I just blurted out Geraldo Rivera when the correct answer was Dr. Phil. I was devastated, because as a college kid, ballin' on a budget, I really could've used that $25 to buy more muffins. I was so embarrassed by my answer that I went on my merry way and never told anyone about the interview. Why the fuck did I say Geraldo Rivera? What a loser-y answer! Years later, the entire series got put on Netflix and my big, bad secret was out.

Television cameos aside, by the end of my first semester, I was starting to get bored: a feeling I'd never imagined I was capable of feeling. My entire life I'd craved boredom. I'd lusted after the idea of having nothing to do. But when it came down to it, boredom was fucking boring! So I brushed my hair, put on my finest pair of Danskin leggings, and decided to get a job.

I felt a lot of pressure to figure my life out. Everyone on campus and in my classes was very career oriented. It seemed like most of the people around me had shown up to freshman orientation with postgrad plans, and some of them even had jobs lined up. I didn't have the same level of focus and planning; all I was focused on was when I was getting another muffin. But after a few months of sleeping in, eating, and watching TV all day, I knew I had to do something productive with my time besides gain weight.

I decided to get an internship to fill my days and, as a bonus, earn a few school credits. So, in February of 2013, a month into my second semester at school, I applied to a few internships in fashion. I scrolled the pages of FreeFashionInternships.com for hours searching for something suitable. Looking back, that was an incredibly strange and out-of-character thing for me to do because I don't really like fashion. I have no pAsSioN 4 fAsHiOn. As an industry, I think it's super noninclusive, and—no shade to Derek Blasberg—I just don't really understand fashion. I pretty much own three shirts and they're all black. So it was an odd field for me to dive into, but I landed an internship at a small e-commerce retail website and I was genuinely excited about the idea of leaving my dorm room three days a week. The internship was unpaid but I figured what I lacked in money, I'd make up for in experience. They accept experience as a form of payment at most clubs, right?

The moment I decided to leave the comfort of my own bed, I immediately regretted it. Working was miserable. Oh my God. I'd never realized how long the days were! Working in corporate America was nothing like Tyra Banks made it seem like in *Life-Size*. After my first day at work, I got on the subway, went back to my dorm room, and fell asleep at seven o'clock. I had never been so tired in my life. I suddenly felt enormous respect for my parents and every adult I knew who had been working their entire life. I immediately knew that working was not going to be my thing. For a little brat like me, that internship opened my eyes to how hard the real world is.

I thought about quitting but was in too deep at the internship to turn back. I had no choice but to stick around and at least try to make it work. The problem was that I was having a hard time making friends with my coworkers and an even harder time doing my job properly. Everyone in my office was really mean and they all ate vegetables for lunch. Just vegetables, not even with a sauce or anything! I couldn't relate to these people whatsoever. They had that stuck-up attitude that seems to radiate throughout the fashion industry. I felt so out of place. For a few weeks I really tried to make it work and blend in. At one point I even bought a pair of metallic sneaker wedges in a last-ditch effort to conform. I was the only intern, I wasn't being paid, and there was no air-conditioning in the small, stuffy office—the latter proved to be a particularly large problem, given the fact that I've been overheating since the day I was born. There were just racks and racks of fast fashion made in Cambodian sweatshops (probably). It was my worst nightmare, personified.

Pretty much the only responsibility I was given as an intern was going into those racks and finding specific items to send out to magazines and publishers for PR. I'd wait around all day for someone to email me a photo of the specific black tank top they were looking for and the serial number associated with it. My job was to find the exact tank top and arrange a messenger to pick it up. The issue was that there were hundreds of borderline-identical black tank tops in the racks, and to my untrained eye, they all looked the same. They were all black and they were all tank tops. I was consistently sending out the wrong shirts to the wrong magazines multiple times a day.

It was defeating and emotionally draining to not only be at the bottom of the totem pole but also feel like I couldn't do anything right. I was drowning in a never-ending sea of black "camisoles," as they called them. It took me a month to realize that "camisole" is just another fucking word for "shirt." Truthfully, I was not a very good intern, mostly because I had a shitty attitude and thought I was too good to be someone's bitch. I didn't understand the need for my job and I hated everyone in the office. They were skinny and mean—a lethal combination.

After each treacherous day at work, I would write these long-winded (and unintentionally hysterical) emails to my family about how miserable I was. It was such a good way for me to blow off steam from the day and kill time before *Breaking Amish* started. They would all laugh and send emojis, and after the first few emails, my mom thought they were so funny, she suggested I start a blog. And for the first time in my life, I listened to my mom.

I started the blog on Tumblr and called it Girl With a Job because I was a girl who had a job. I wasn't exactly the most clever intern on the planet, but the title made sense at the time. I wanted to write about my experiences as the office bitch. The blog served as a creative outlet for me to write diary entries complaining about my day, my bosses, and, frankly, having to work at all. It wasn't made for anyone to see. I'd refer to bosses and co-workers using ridiculous nicknames for them. It was the perfect outlet for my rage. It was mostly just for me, but I shared it with a few friends here and there. I decided to keep it anonymous because it was more of a diary than a blog and if any of my coworkers found it, I would've been sent to HR and fired immediately.

Even though nobody was actually reading my blog, I *adored* the art of blogging and referring to myself as a blogger. Nowadays, everyone and their mother has a blog. But in 2013, having a blog was a very cool and cutting-edge thing to do. I felt like I had found my calling. Which is why I was completely devastated when I made the decision to delete GWAJ. I was tired of coming into work every day petrified that someone would find my blog, even though, again, not a single person was reading it. I cringed at the notion of my boss reading a blog post where I lovingly referred to her as "Granny" simply because she was the oldest person in the office. That mental image was enough to make me delete my entire blog forever.

That spring, as I neared the end of the school year, I ended up getting let go from the internship when they said they didn't need me anymore. I think I really fucked the whole thing up when I was asked to order lunch for the entire office on the day of a big photo shoot. I never clicked "submit" when placing the massive order for the crew. After two hours, everyone was hounding me about where lunch was. When I realized I'd never actually placed the order, I knew it wouldn't be long before they fired my ass. It was the last straw. Before you feel bad for me, let me tell you: I had never felt more free. Getting fired was the best day of my life. I was no longer locked up in the shackles of corporate America. I could go back to sleeping in, and more important, I could start blogging again.

It's funny when I think back on the start of my career, because as a college student, I could barely put two words together when it came to essays or research papers. But when it came to blogging, I was endlessly inspired. I ended up changing the name to Girl With No Job, to more accurately reflect where I was in my life. I was no longer anonymous, so instead of talking shit about my coworkers, my blog posts now documented the life of a millennial college student. I created a fictionalized version of my life. I slowly constructed an overly dramatized character around my real self. Lots of what I blogged wasn't true, but it was funny, and that was all I cared about. Then I started transitioning into writing about more universal topics and that's when things got interesting. I blogged about how long I could go without shaving my legs and the intricacies of getting the best manicure in New York. Groundbreaking stuff.

After a while, the blog wasn't really about me anymore; it was more universal. The minute I took my head out of my own ass and started writing about more relatable things, the blog began to gain traction. I was blissfully unaware of politically correct culture and I didn't care. I didn't want to be woke, I just wanted to be funny— no matter the cost. That would later come back to haunt me.

In the fall of my sophomore year, after a few more months of blogging, I took to platforms like Facebook and Twitter to promote GWNJ. People were actually starting to take note; more and more people were reading the blog every day. I even got the chance to interview celebrities like Ryan Cabrera (post–Audrina Patridge) and Penn Badgley (post–*Gossip Girl*, pre-*You*).

Social media had become an amazing and effective resource for me to promote my blog. I had a personal Instagram account at the time that I used to post overedited photos of me and my friends just like everyone else I knew, but I had seen a few people join the platform to promote their brands/blogs and I thought it could be a great way for me to do the same. I ended up making a second Instagram account for Girl With No Job. I wanted to get my name out there, and since I was too lazy to get out of bed, Instagram was the next best thing. I never intended to start a business on Instagram. If anything, I thought it could help me achieve an ounce of fame, which has always been priority number one. Once I experienced the thrill of posting on Instagram and getting that immediate feedback from my audience, I was hooked. I knew there was a real opportunity there to expand my business and create a community of people from all around the world. I ended up creating a whole new brand on Instagram and slowly left my blog behind.

My following continued to grow throughout college. My Instagram content was funny and relatable, and the minute I posted, people were sending it to their friends. Then their friends would follow me and send my stuff to their other friends. People were keeping in touch with their school and camp friends in my comments section.

I was spending all my time trying to grow my Instagram. I was capitalizing on pivotal pop culture moments and making content out of them. I was using every hashtag imaginable to make my account discoverable. I had about three hundred thousand followers when I got my first sponsorship, during the summer of 2014, right after my sophomore year. Burger King was running a campaign to promote the return of their famous Chicken Fries, and their agency offered me $1,000 to create content about it for my Instagram. I gladly accepted their offer. I had never had that much money in my bank account before. I immediately ran to Space Market to spend my fortune.

I changed my major from physics to media and communications with the hope that my coursework would support my new career path, or at least give me something to fall back on that was related to what I was already doing. Girl With No Job was growing and I was being offered opportunities I could only dream of—getting paid by brands, walking on red carpets, taking expensive trips. I was even asked to appear on a digital episode of Nicole Richie's reality show *Candidly Nicole*. Unfortunately, the shoot date was the same day as my sister Margo's high school graduation. Suffice it to say I never made it to her graduation. The opportunities being thrown my way were exciting and confusing all at the same time. I wasn't entirely sure what was happening but I decided to run with it.

It was difficult at times to be a full-time student while trying to grow my business. I would constantly miss classes for meetings or trips. And trying to explain my Instagram business to my professors, in 2014, was not exactly an easy task. But by my senior year, Girl With No Job was my sole source of income, so I had no choice but to keep going. It was awkward for me to have to explain to my classmates and professors what I was doing after school and why I had to cut out early. These days, if a student were in my position, I think their professor would *kind of* understand it, but back then, nobody understood what the fuck I was doing on my laptop all day.

Even though my academic life was falling apart, I was somehow always present and accounted for when it came to my social life. I had my priorities in order. I felt like the social scene in college prepared me more for real life than any of my courses did. I had a fun group of friends and I rarely missed a night out. I was a proud club rat, and NYU was the ideal place for me to perfect the art of clubbing. I loved going out and getting drunk. It's how I met my husband.

As my business grew, I felt like Hannah Montana, living a double life. At barely twenty years old, I was building a brand online that was turning into a pretty lucrative, successful business. At the same time, I was going to classes, turning in assignments, and hanging out with my friends like a regular college kid. It was a strange experience to balance these two worlds, and I never wanted them to meet. I was kind of embarrassed by Girl With No Job. I was telling my followers things I'd never even told my friends. I was afraid people wouldn't get it, so I never let my two worlds collide.

This was a particularly difficult task when I got my first press opportunity. I was interviewed for a popular Swedish news program called *Kobra*. It wasn't exactly the *Today* show but I was excited nonetheless. I didn't really understand why they wanted to interview me, because I wasn't exactly big in Sweden, but I am never one to turn down an opportunity to be on TV, even if it wasn't in English. The production crew offered to send a car to pick me up from my dorm. Imagine my horror when an enormous gray stretch limousine pulled up in front of Weinstein Residence Hall. Everyone stared at me like I had two heads as I slid my way into the limo. I was mortified.

The interview went well. I think. They drove me around campus, interviewing me in the back of what looked like a limo from *The Godfather*. The interviewer spoke English but the entire segment aired in Swedish, so I'm not entirely sure what was said about me, but I looked cute and that's all I really cared about at the time.

The biggest challenge I faced in keeping my two worlds separate was a course I took called Social Media Networking during my junior year. I took the class because I thought it would be an easy A. I had cracked the code of social media, so how hard could a college class on it be? Well, really hard, apparently. The entire class was a joke. I was living on social media, so reading about it in textbooks seemed silly to me. My professor was very serious and rigid, and she clearly did not like me. I felt like I should've been teaching the class. That might explain why she didn't like me. She gave us a journaling assignment that required us to document our activity on social media for a week. I didn't know how I could have done the assignment without including the fact that, at the time, I had five hundred thousand Instagram followers and was running a business based entirely on Instagram.

I decided to reference Girl With No Job *once* in the assignment. I was sure my professor would have some follow-up questions and I was prepared to answer them. I got the assignment back; I had gotten a C+. I quickly flipped to page 3, where I mentioned my Instagram account. She had circled it and written, "WHAT IS THIS?" The class ended up being a big waste of my time.

It felt even more like a waste when I made my American television debut just a few weeks after turning in that flop of an assignment. When a producer from *Steve Harvey* reached out to me, I knew that the whole Instagram thing might be something more than a hobby. The show was huge at the time. I got an email from a producer who was working on a dating segment featuring people with big social followings. They were looking for *single* people to feature on the show and set up with potential suitors, based solely on their social media profiles. I responded immediately, saying I would love to come on and that I was single when, actually, Ben and I were very seriously dating. At that point we'd been together for almost two years, and I'd finally bullied him into a serious and committed relationship (I'll fill you in on the full story later). I thought Ben would be furious at me for wanting to go on national television as a single girl, but he understood and respected my thirst for fame, and that's why I love him.

NBC flew me out to Chicago for my very first live TV appearance. It was such a big deal. The entire Jewish community of the Upper East Side had their DVRs set. I was stoked and, shockingly, not nervous. I brought Ben with me and told everyone on set that he was my brother. Nobody questioned it. In hindsight, that's kind of alarming.

I got the "script" the night before the taping when production sent it to my hotel room. I remember reading it while in the bathtub and then proceeding to have a mental breakdown.

I didn't understand why I needed a script. It made no sense. It was a talk show, not a soap opera! And the way they wrote all my lines made me sound like a sixty-year-old man trying to talk to his grandchildren. I decided to toss the script and just be myself. After all, wasn't that why they wanted me?

They didn't let me meet Steve until I sat down for the segment. He didn't address me directly until we were live and on-air. I'm sure if I watched the segment back now, I'd cringe. I was trying really hard to be cool and not look nervous when in reality, my Spanx were soaked in sweat. I was also wearing the lamest outfit: a Ted Baker blouse and pencil skirt that made me look like the rabbi's wife on a High Holiday.

Ultimately I was paired up with a lovely young man whom I never saw again. I want to say his name was Joe.

I felt great after we wrapped. I thought I was very funny and sassy, and I think Steve liked me more than he'd thought he would. I think he was impressed by this short, plump Jewish girl who was outspoken, funny, and kind of nuts. After we finished taping the show, he turned to me, grabbed me by the shoulders, and said: "You're going to be a star." It was very cliché but I loved every minute of it. Getting that kind of validation from someone at the top of his game in the industry made me feel like I could make something of myself.

Steve was so impressed with me that after the taping, he asked me to connect with his social team, led by his step-daughter, to give them some of my thoughts on how to manage and grow his social media. I sat down and wrote out tons of ideas for his content strategy and how to ultimately expand his following. I made a content calendar and everything! I was honored that Steve considered me a professional and I didn't want to let him down. A few weeks later we all got on a conference call and I could tell that none of them were thrilled to hear from me. I think I came off a little too eager to tell them what they were all doing wrong. That was the last time we all spoke, lol.

The whole experience on *Steve Harvey* was a real game changer for me. My confidence in what I could do and where Girl With No Job could take me was through the roof, as if my head couldn't get any bigger. Plus, I got six thousand new followers from the appearance. I was on my way.

Right before I graduated, I got another big break when I appeared as the guest bartender on *Watch What Happens Live*. As a (somewhat serious) joke, I had created a Change.org petition demanding that Bravo let me bartend an episode. My Instagram had a big enough following that Bravo saw the petition, thought it was hilarious, and invited me on the show.

I couldn't believe I had actually gotten myself booked on a real late-night TV show. It was a huge moment for me and the first time I thought: *Oh, I could be famous. Not just a girl with an Instagram account, but an actual famous person.*

The experience was incredible! I had an amazing time, and

Andy Cohen was everything I'd dreamed he would be. His love for Bravo and reality TV wasn't just for show. He was as genuine and passionate about his work as you would want him to be. I sent him an email after the show, thanking him profusely for having me on. As such a big fan of him and his work, I wanted him to know how grateful I was for the opportunity. I also wanted to be invited back. Which I was, a year later, for a *Watch What Happens Live* Social Media Week event. I got to interview Andy for the *WWHL* after-show and it was fabulous. I was an even bigger Andy fan than before, had read all his books, and knew the key to his heart was weed. I knew that this was my moment, but as someone who doesn't smoke, I had no idea where to get weed. Pot? What do the kids call it these days?

I'd asked one of Ben's friends to roll me a joint, which I'd thrown in my wallet, and before Andy left the event I asked if he wanted to smoke. He said sure. I was *trembling*. We went out on the terrace of the *Watch What Happens Live* studio and lit up a doobie. I had no intention of actually getting high but I pretended to inhale. We chatted mostly about housewives and the weather. He smoked most of the poorly rolled joint. I was ecstatic that my plan worked. I realize this story makes me sound like a loser, but I don't care. I wanted to be able to say that I'd smoked pot with Andy Cohen, and now I can.

I couldn't believe the Change.org petition worked. It made a monster out of me. Now I make petitions for things I want and it usually works. In 2018, I made a petition to save *Friends* because they were taking it off Netflix. It got over a hundred thousand signatures and tons of press, and it ended up keeping *Friends* on Netflix for a whole other year. Netflix paid a hundred million dollars to keep it on for one more year.

By my senior year of college, I was pretty much checked out of school. In addition to running Girl With No Job, I also was interning three days a week at AOL. I know it sounds nuts, given how much I had on my plate, but I still wasn't entirely sure that Girl With No Job was going to be a stable enough business for me after graduation. In 2016, nobody was a full-time "influencer"; it just wasn't a thing. I needed a backup plan, and that's what AOL was for me. It was an amazing place to intern and it had full-time-job-offer potential. In between school, GWNJ, and TV appearances, I sat at my desk and ran the social media for one of AOL's verticals.

The internship at AOL was the kind of internship that almost always turns into a full-time job offer. I landed the job during that time in college where everyone around you is landing full-time jobs and launching their careers. Anyone in my position would've been so grateful for that internship and definitely would have tried to turn it into a job.

Under any other circumstances, I would have loved to work there. It was a huge media company and there were so many opportunities for me to grow there. Both my older sisters had landed full-time jobs there after college as well. But I really wanted to see what I could do with Girl With No Job without the added pressures of school and work. Plus, I just couldn't see the point in taking a job making $30,000 a year when one campaign with E! paid me that much. It was just so silly. So I turned down the job offer and the coveted health care package that came along with it.

I graduated by the skin of my teeth. I was even placed on academic probation at one point. I handed in most of my assignments, but I was never really present. It had dawned on me, for a moment, that I didn't need to graduate to pursue my career. It sure would've made my life easier, but I recognized how big a privilege it is to go to college, and I was going to graduate no matter what. I just wasn't raised that way, to be so reckless. People love to say, "Bill Gates didn't graduate college!" and while that may be true, there are also a million other people who had big dreams, dropped out of college, and did nothing with their lives. I was not about to be one of those morons.

At graduation, I was one of the only people I knew who wasn't going straight into working full-time. I wasn't going to medical school, I wasn't going to law school. I was going to become a star. It was every parent's worst nightmare.

CHAPTER THREE

Girl With No Full-Time Job

After graduation, life as a full-time Girl With No Job wasn't exactly what I'd dreamed it would be. I thought I would be running around town, kicking ass and making deals. I thought I'd constantly be jetting off to events and red carpets. But postgrad life wasn't anything like that. I didn't want to admit it at the time, but it was kind of boring. So much of being Girl With No Job required me to be a girl without a job. So that's what I was. I spent my days making content from my bed and answering emails from my couch. I slept till noon, watched reality TV, and got paid for it. It was the golden age of reality TV and I was watching everything and recapping it on my Instagram. Characters from the *Real Housewives*,

Vanderpump Rules, and *The Bachelor* became my only friends as I lay at home "working." It was easy work but it wasn't fulfilling. I was making a lot of money for a postgrad media major, but my life lacked any real structure.

I took the next few months to get my shit together. Filed trademarks, started a corporation, paid my taxes! I didn't want to end up in jail like a washed-up reality star who forgot to file their W-2. There was so much I didn't know about making money. Success is amazing, but it's really dangerous if you don't know what you're doing. You can get yourself into a lot of trouble. Early on, I made the responsible decision to hire both a lawyer and an accountant so as not to screw things up. I was constantly surrounded by people reminding me not to mess with the IRS. But in the words of Hannah Montana, "nobody's perfect." I had to deal with my fair share of fuck-ups when it came to legitimizing my business. I had to, on more than one occasion, pay back taxes for money I'd made in college. That was terrifying. The IRS sent their notices in certified-mail envelopes that pretty much made me shit my pants on the spot. I opened a notice, saw the five-figure amount that I owed, and immediately envisioned what my life would be like if I had to go to prison. I called my accountant crying. He assured me that this happens to a lot of people, especially entertainers. He even let me know that tons of his celebrity clients were on payment plans to the government.

That made me feel a little better, but I was still freaking out. My biggest fear in life is going to prison. I have recurring nightmares about it. I watch too much *Law & Order*. I don't look good in orange, and I'd probably be the first person in history to somehow get fat in prison.

The first year after I graduated in 2016 was a sort of master class in running my own business. I learned the basic financial and legal components, but perhaps more important, I finally had to harness my work ethic and keep myself on track with deadlines. I was negotiating all my own deals with brands and agencies, and learning the ins and outs of running a successful influencer marketing campaign. Through trial and error, I began to master how to advocate for myself and know my value in the always unstable influencer economy. There was, and still is, no real financial standard when it comes to influencing. I learned what I can and should be charging brands for my work and how to get them to agree to it.

After a year of being Girl with No Full-Time Job, I had the opportunity to go back to AOL and take a meeting with the CEO of the company. I was scared shitless, so I begged my sisters to join me in the meeting since they were both still full-time employees at AOL. AOL had just been acquired by Verizon and merged with Yahoo!. They were acquiring companies and apps constantly, so naturally, I thought they wanted to meet with me because they wanted to acquire the Girl With

No Job brand. It was an insanely unrealistic expectation but crazier things have happened.

Unfortunately, that wasn't the case. In the meeting, the executives explained that they were looking for young, forward-thinking creators to do something innovative and fresh for their—how do I say this nicely?—*antiquated* company. They had watched my community grow on Instagram since my time as an intern and they wanted in. They asked if we would be interested in coming up with concepts for young, cool digital brands for Verizon to launch. Even though we had no ideas yet, we said yes.

The three of us immediately started brainstorming ideas that could potentially take off. We were sitting in a conference room eating Goldfish and drinking Diet Coke when a lightbulb went off. Jackie and I had had this fixation with morning shows ever since we saw *Morning Glory*, the heartwarming comedy starring Rachel McAdams. We'd been holding on to the idea of an entertainment morning show, hosted by Jackie and me, named *The Morning Breath*. The name itself was too funny not to try. As a natural born momager, Olivia was the perfect person to fill the role of our producer. So that's what we pitched. And surprisingly, the bigwigs loved it. We didn't want to commit to waking up at four a.m. every day, so we decided on a midmorning show, going live at ten thirty a.m.

Verizon had multiple TV and digital studios in both their Manhattan offices. They had state-of-the-art cameras and sets, none of which we were allowed to use. We ended up livestreaming from an old iPhone in an empty corner office. Not exactly state-of-the-art. Olivia took two iPhones, one for Instagram Live and one for Facebook Live, and held them in her hands for as long as she could while Jackie and I sat there delivering the top pop culture news. Low budget? Yes. Boring? Never.

After our first episode, elated from all the positive feedback from the audience, we got a strongly worded email from the Verizon legal team. Apparently, the empty office we had been sequestered in had a mural on the wall made up of album covers; streaming it was a copyright infringement. We had to find a new "set" immediately. Which we did. We got permission to use an old studio space in the back of the building for an hour a day. It wasn't glamorous, by any means, but it was good enough to get us started.

After six months, we demanded to be taken more seriously. And by "we," I mean Olivia. She embraced her inner Kris Jenner and demanded we get access to the proper resources. She got us an hour on the main set, right before Yahoo! Finance went live. We had a full AV staff, six audio and camera technicians, working on our show, and it felt like we had arrived.

Our show became so popular online that after only a few months, Verizon decided to formally pick it up and offered us a budget. If there's one thing I never turn down, it's a budget. Well, two things: I also never turn down a pastry. Verizon gave us money to spend internally on launching the show. The money was to be used for staff, equipment, and a small salary for each of us. Jackie and I didn't have agents or managers to negotiate the deal for us, and we barely read the agreement before signing it. We were eager to get started; the logistics weren't of importance to us. Which, in the words of Julia Roberts, was a big mistake. Huge!

At first it was kind of sickening to be at a company like Verizon. I was twenty-one years old, producing and starring in a show with my sisters on someone else's dime. We were living out our dreams, getting paid to do it, and we weren't risking anything. If it failed, we could wash our hands and walk away. But working at Verizon wasn't always ideal. We were very limited in the ancillary ways we could expand our business while under the regime of corporate America. We tried to release a line of *Morning Breath* merch but were immediately shut down by legal, yet again. We were also forced to censor ourselves quite a bit even though the show was branded as a completely unfiltered morning show. When we alluded to the shady behavior of a certain producer at another network, we were required to take a two-hour course on compliance and what is considered defamation. I'd never been so bored in my life. Apparently, everything that's ever come out of my mouth can be considered defamatory or libelous. (Kidding, of course.)

In the beginning, nobody at the company gave a shit about us. They had no idea what we were doing from ten thirty to eleven thirty a.m. But after a year, *The Morning Breath* had become a shining star in the Verizon portfolio. Our numbers were growing, and we had tons of celebrity talent coming on. Publicists were reaching out to *us* to get their celebrity clients on our show. People were sliding into my DMs on Instagram asking to come on. It was unbelievable. We had Barbara Corcoran, Ramona Singer, and even Rob Gronkowski come on the show. To the old men upstairs at Verizon HQ, that was all they needed to hear. They agreed to renegotiate our contracts. We weren't making much money from the show, but once we proved the concept to Verizon, we knew they'd fork over the cash. As *The Morning Breath* had gained traction, I had been signed as a client at Creative Artists Agency and now had a fancy digital talent agent to renegotiate my contract. Payday was around the corner.

Days before I was supposed to sign my new contract, filled with a healthy salary, health care, and stock options, Verizon cancelled *The Morning Breath* due to the fact that I, in fact, was cancelled. Ah yes, the Tonya Harding to my Nancy Kerrigan–esque rise to glory. More on that saga later, but suffice it to say: it took me out at the knees, though not for long. And my payday never arrived.

The Morning Breath aired for about a year. It was an incredible experience, mostly because I loved working with Jackie and

Olivia so much. It changed the course of my career forever, and as much as I'd like to think back on that time negatively, given how it ended, I am really grateful for the experience and the path it eventually put me on. The year I spent there helped me convert my Instagram audience from followers into fans. Thanks to our show, they were getting to know the girl behind the memes. They knew Claudia, the girl behind Girl With No Job. That's what I had always wanted.

The last episode of *The Morning Breath* aired on February 28, 2018. On April 9, 2018, four weeks after the cancellation, Jackie and I launched *The Morning Toast*. And as they say, the rest is history. I would've preferred to stay on hiatus for much more than a month. I was not ready to face the world but I needed to work. I had no money coming in and the bills were piling up. I owed tens of thousands of dollars to lawyers, crisis managers, and publicists whom I had hired during the fallout. I really had no choice but to come back. Our numbers tripled upon premiere. Most of our listeners from *The Morning Breath* welcomed us back into their lives with open arms. And whether we liked it or not, the surge of bad press we'd received not four weeks earlier made us interesting. People who had never heard of us nor our show now knew who we were, and some of them wanted to know more. They say all press is good press and while that was proving to be true, I wasn't comfortable with it. I wasn't exactly thrilled to be known for my worst moment.

In the years since we launched, we have expanded our brand tremendously and even created our own podcast network, Toast News Network. We saw how our listeners were desperate for content, and even though we were churning out five episodes a week, we knew they wanted more. We decided to create the network so that we could not only give a platform to our favorite influencers, celebrities, and reality stars but also give our audience more of what they want—content. The audience has and always will be the focus of our brand. I like to think of *The Morning Toast* as a catering company. We cater constantly to the needs and demands of our audience. They wanted more content, we gave them more content. They wanted live events, we gave them live events.

With *The Morning Toast* and our five-day-a-week schedule, I finally got the structure I had so craved in the early days of Girl With No Job. And, more important, I felt like my work had purpose. I felt like I was contributing something positive to the world, even if it was only for an hour a day. I felt like I could sleep well at night knowing that my work meant something to someone. Having seen the impact of our *Morning Toast* community has cemented that feeling for me. People rely on the show; it's a part of their routine and part of what informs the way they see the world, at least the pop culture world. I am really proud of that. A lot of the listeners use the show as an escape from the troubles of their daily lives. It may seem like a relatively unimportant show to an outsider, but if you're a part of the community, then you know that it's actually the opposite.

The community, which was cultivated entirely by the listeners, continues to blow my mind. Toasters, as they proudly call themselves, are taking their Internet relationships into the real world. They're meeting fellow Toasters in their cities and creating lifelong friendships. They're spending their Memorial Day weekends with relative strangers in the Pocono Mountains at Camp Toast—a weekend dedicated to celebrating our community. None of that would've happened if it weren't for our show.

I've been really shocked at the impact our show has had on our audience. To me, it's a fun part of my job. But to the regular viewers, it's an important part of their day. Meeting our listeners in real life has been eye-opening for me. When I did a comedy show in Miami, these two sisters came up to me at the meet-and-greet and they said, "You know, we've had this kind of strained relationship, but we both started watching *The Morning Toast* and it really brought us so much closer." They had tears in their eyes when they said it to me, and I started sobbing. Nobody's ever said something that nice to me. And as someone who comes from such a tight-knit family, I knew *exactly* what they were talking about. That was really special. It's amazing to think of the impact of a social media account I started in college.

I attribute much of our success with *The Morning Toast* and Toast News Network to the fact that Jackie and I are sisters. So much of our on-air dynamic and banter is rooted in our sisterly bond. We can be real and tough with each other, the way that only sisters can be. There's nothing we won't say to each other. We don't have to tiptoe around anything. We speak a common language and our viewers really respond to that. Our public sisterhood makes strangers feel like they're a part of our family, and now they are.

The success of *The Morning Toast* didn't happen overnight. Five hundred episodes later, we've carved out a sizable audience for ourselves. But it wasn't without lots of hard work and difficulty. It's not easy to go on-air and talk for an hour every day without making a fair share of mistakes. We are an unedited, unfiltered show, which leaves a lot of room for trial and error.

The success of the show has allowed us to expand not only our brand but also our roster of guests. Because we have such a big audience, celebrities want to get in on it when they're promoting projects. We were even contacted by the White House to have Dr. Deborah Birx from the Coronavirus Task Force on the show to speak directly to millennials. It was an honor to be recognized by the government as a major news source for millennial women.

The guests are my favorite part of doing the show, not only because I am a proud star fucker and social climber but also because it's cool to get to speak with people whom we would normally be speaking *about*. It's so meta! We get to hear straight from them on stories we would report on. And some of them are so cool, you can't help but fall in love with them. Jerry O'Connell stayed at the studio for forty-five minutes gossiping with us about all the drama that goes down in his hometown of Calabasas. He even divulged a couple of stories about his wife, Rebecca Romijn's, experience filming an episode of *Friends* back in the day. And let me tell you, the tea was piping hot.

It's been really empowering and fulfilling to build a business where I get to be my own boss, make my own hours, and hire other people, which is something I never thought I would do. The Internet has given me the opportunity to grow into a businesswoman and teach myself how to advocate on my own behalf, which is very difficult to do, especially as a young woman. Early on, I had to deal with a lot of people not taking me seriously, mostly because of the way I look and the way I talk. I say "like" a lot and I'm barely five feet tall. That doesn't exactly scream "serious businesswoman." But I demanded to be taken seriously because I am serious as fuck! I wouldn't have been able to do that if it weren't for social media. I would have graduated college and ended up in some dead-end job where I'd want to kill my coworkers. Instagram gave me the opportunity to become an entrepreneur without having to go on *Shark Tank*.

I have found the Internet to be one of the most fulfilling places. Of course, it has its downfalls (hi, trolls. I am sure you picked up this book to make fun of it!), but social media gave me the courage to be something I never thought I would be—a businesswoman and a leader. I learned, and am still learning, so much about what it means to be a public figure and the responsibilities that come with that. I don't always say the right thing, and it's something I work on daily, but if it weren't for that little, irrelevant blog I started in 2013, I wouldn't be the person, the wife, or the sister I am now.

It's weird to think about how vast the Internet is, filled with so much information and nonsense, but it's also allowed us to cultivate new and vibrant communities where we can make each other laugh and lift each other up. Everyone can find a place for themselves, whether you love pop culture or you get your rocks off watching videos of pimples getting popped (guilty as charged). There's truly something for everyone.

CHAPTER FOUR

In Search Of: Nice Jewish Boy With No Job

I've been married for three years and in a serious relationship for seven, and if I've learned anything it's that I should've gotten married *earlier*. I know that may sound insane because everybody already thinks I'm an Amish freak for having gotten married at twenty-three. But having a significant other is everything of the sort. Maybe it relates to my fear of being alone, but the moment I got into a serious relationship, I loved the idea that I had someone to hang out with all the time. Ben Soffer, my husband, was my first serious relationship if you don't count my summer romance at Jewish sleepaway camp. He's also the only man I've ever had sex with, so I kind of understand why people think I'm an Amish freak. I didn't plan on only having sex with one person but I met Ben when I was eighteen, things just worked out that way, and I am not mad about it.

Ben is the person for me, I have no doubt about that. We're similar in all the ways we should be but our differences complement each other. I think if I were to ever look into it, Ben and I are probably related. I have people message me regularly, telling me that after following me for years they *just* realized that Ben and I are not siblings. I don't blame them! We have very similar Eastern European Ashkenazi Jewish backgrounds, we look like each other, and we have so many of the same personality traits. I just know we're related but am too afraid to look into it because if I found out that I've been having sex with a distant relative for the last seven years, I'd jump off a cliff.

When Ben and I first started dating, officially, I was obsessed with having a boyfriend. I told anyone who would listen about him. I quickly became that girl constantly saying, "My boyfriend this, my boyfriend that . . . ," and when we got engaged that just got worse. I had a fiancé and everybody needed to know it. I had never had a boyfriend before Ben, and I was proud that I had gotten one. A good one, too. That's no easy feat. We did everything together and I was hell-bent on documenting it on social media. Once I had a boyfriend, everyone on Instagram had to know about it. It was nonstop. I'm not even ashamed. I loved the idea that he hung out with me because he wanted to, not because he had to, like my sisters. He thought I was funny and pretty, and that made me love myself even more. He believed in me so much and always made me feel important and special. If someone as cute and eligible as Ben loved me, how could I not love myself?

My life totally changed when Ben came into the picture. The days of sending group texts every Saturday night asking where the party was were gone. My relationship was the party! I stopped caring what everyone else was doing and if people were hanging out without me. I was too busy making out with Ben to care. He let me squeeze his blackheads, and that made me feel like the luckiest girl in the world.

I guess I should tell you guys how we met because it's a great story. And even though Ben was my first (and last) boyfriend *and* I've only ever been on one date in my whole life, I consider myself a dating expert because it clearly went well.

It was the spring of 2013 and I was an overly confident, chunky NYU freshman. Looking back, I was actually really skinny, because I'm super chubby now. Back then, I thought I was the fattest bitch on campus, but right now I would literally give up my right arm to be at the weight I was then. It's weird how numbers work. Maybe in a few years, I will look back at photos from this year and think I was so thin. What a frightening thought.

Anyway, if you know anything about NYU, you know it's not exactly the most fun school in the country. It doesn't have a football team or any real social scene. While most college freshmen spend their Thursday nights blacking out at frat houses, I was planning on watching *Friends* and eating Baked Cheetos until I fell asleep. I had heard about a party that I had no interest in going to, but I ultimately fell into the peer pressure that is FOMO and got dressed.

I arrived at the party as I do most places: late and disinterested. I beelined straight for the bar and then found a nice place to sit by the air-conditioning so I wouldn't start sweating too much (side note: wow, I really have not changed). After spending an hour in the corner with my friends, quietly judging everyone who walked by, someone new and unfamiliar arrived. Now, I know I make it seem like I'm antisocial—and I am—but trust me when I say that I know every single Jewish person in the New York/tristate area. If I meet you and pretend I don't know who you are, I'm just being a bitch. I've seen your Facebook and Instagram and I know you went to Aruba last summer with your cousins. So imagine my surprise when I saw a cute, beefy Jewish boy, wearing a Ferragamo belt, and had no clue who he was.

I am many things but subtle is not one of them. I walked straight up to Ben and we had the shortest, weirdest, most awkward conversation of all time. Of course, I thought it went great and thought that he would 100 percent text me the next day. Spoiler alert: he didn't.

When I didn't wake up to a marriage proposal via text, I was horrified to say the least. But never underestimate a GWNJ in love. I got on my computer and did some research on this Ben fellow. We had a mutual friend, whom I obviously reached out to and forced to talk Ben into asking me out. Which he did. So romantic, I know.

Fast-forward to the night of our date. I almost threw up while getting ready. I was so fucking nervous but it was beyond the classic first-date jitters. We were going to get drinks at a local bar. The issue was that I was only eighteen while Ben was twenty-one and legally allowed to drink. I couldn't stop imagining my fake ID getting rejected at the bar. I kept visualizing myself getting taken away in handcuffs. I just knew that it would really pinpoint how immature I was. The awkwardness of that visual put a pit in my stomach the size of Texas.

Luckily, that did not happen, and the second I successfully ordered my drink I finally let loose and stopped being such a freak. We had a great date. Really textbook fantastic. If I could write a book about the perfect first date, this would be it. We had rapid-fire banter and a flirty, casual rapport. Sparks were literally flying. Except for one tiny tiny tiny tiny tiny minuscule thing. At one point, Ben did mention that he was not looking for anything serious or long-term. He mentioned he had recently gotten out of a serious relationship and was just looking to have fun. I was heartbroken but mostly confused. If you're not looking to date anyone, THEN DON'T TAKE ANYONE ON A FUCKING DATE.

So I did what any normal, sane girl would do in that type of situation. I completely ignored it, pursued him as my boyfriend, and continued to be shocked and upset when he didn't respond in the way that I wanted him to. At one point, I think I actually referred to him as my boyfriend to some of my friends. I treated him like my boyfriend. I texted him every morning and we made out almost every night. It was the dream relationship, except one of us didn't know the relationship had started.

Ben eventually grew tired of my acting like a total nut job and ended things with me after a few weeks. And, as you can imagine, I was devastated. Like, totally and completely heartbroken. I kept staring at my phone, thinking he'd text me saying that he had made a huge mistake and wanted to marry me. I thought of nothing but Ben for weeks. I listened to Taylor Swift's *Red* album on repeat since she was the only person who could understand what I was going through. I must have listened to "All Too Well" a thousand times.

In an attempt to get my mind off of things, I threw myself into my studies. Kidding. I threw myself into bed and turned my phone off for a while. The constant anxiety of checking my phone was driving me wild. I know it sounds dramatic to be that upset over a guy whom I had only gone on a few "dates" with at this point, but I had a feeling about him.

I did a lot of self-reflecting over the next few weeks and came to terms with the fact that I was insane and I would end up alone if I didn't get my act together. I vowed to stop all communication with Ben, which freed up a significant amount of my time. With all this new free time, I threw myself into GirlWithNoJob.com and was stunned to find that when you don't text boys first, they might—just might—text you first. And he did. He didn't say anything memorable, he was simply checking in and saying hello. I couldn't believe it. So simple, yet so brilliant. I didn't answer for hours or sometimes days at a time. It was hard, trust me. All I wanted to do was respond in essays and poems telling him how much I missed him, but I held back.

Two weeks later I ran into him at a club, looking snatched to the gods. The next day he asked me to be his girlfriend. Labels and everything. And since then, I've never once doubted Ben's commitment to me or our relationship. I recently found out Ben was invited to that party in college to be set up with the girl who was hosting it. Sorry, Yael. You snooze, you lose.

People are fascinated by my and Ben's relationship because it goes against everything *Sex and the City* taught us. Guys almost never change their ways or their opinions of a girl. If he thinks you're crazy, that's it. But I defied all the odds and got Ben to see me for who I *really* was, not the psychotic overtexter he *thought* I was.

We were both raised Jewish, with similar observances, traditions, and values, give or take. Ben is more serious about Judaism and a little bit more religious than me. He keeps our family on course, which I love. I am more religious now than when I was a kid and I want to keep moving in that direction. I've always wanted to adopt more religious practices and become a little more observant, and Ben really keeps me on track. We keep kosher in our home, which means we only eat kosher meat and never mix meat and dairy. We also try to observe Shabbat at home. For me, going on tour made keeping Shabbat really tough, so I've gotten really off track with that. I'm getting back to it recently, and when we have a family, we plan on being totally observant (famous last words).

I was so happy with Ben because there was an equal amount of excitement and genuine happiness from both of us. He liked me just as much as I liked him, maybe even more. Ben made it clear from the second we started officially dating that he had every intention of proposing and it was just a matter of time. It was always a matter of when, not if. I never questioned our future together, and that security was such a comfort. I didn't have to worry about dating, getting heartbroken, spending time and energy on meeting people and giving them a chance. I hate the concept of dating because you're essentially acting for ninety minutes. Acting like you chew with your mouth closed, acting like you're not crazy. Going on one first date was enough experience for me. Dating is exhausting and I was relieved to not have to deal with it. I was so happy to be in a relationship with someone I loved and, more important, with someone who loved me back.

Even though we were very committed early on, we weren't in a rush. There were a lot of girls in the Jewish community at NYU who would come to class with engagement rings. And it was weird. My mom had told me in no uncertain terms that I wasn't allowed to get engaged until I graduated college. She wanted me to enjoy college and not rush into adulthood.

Our families were very supportive of our relationship. The first time I met Ben's parents, we were on our way out for the evening and he told me to stop by his parents' place first to meet them. Thank goodness that, given my body type, I've never been the type of girl who fucks with crop tops. I looked presentable for his parents even though we were heading out to meet friends after. I was wearing my favorite jacket at the time, an army camouflage coat with leather sleeves that I had stolen from my dreaded fashion internship. Ben's parents had a cute little cocktail hour with hors d'oeuvres, and we just talked, ate, and drank. And then we left. It was very normal and lovely.

Ben's dad, Bruce, is a chef and had prepared all these fabulous hors d'oeuvres for us. But having the palate of a six-year-old made this seemingly normal evening a challenge. At the time, I was on a strict diet of chicken nuggets and French fries. I still am. Bruce had prepared lamb chops and fucking escargot. I was nibbling at the food and doing my best to be sociable and respectful. It's so rude to be in someone's house and not eat their food, especially when the person is a chef. But I couldn't get down with the spread. Thankfully, I have my strategies from a lifetime of pretending to like other people's cooking. I broke up the food on my plate and moved it around. Plus, I gave a little to Ben, too. Then I offered to help with the dishes so I not only looked like a lady but also could throw away my scraps without anyone realizing I hadn't eaten.

The fact that I got engaged right after college and married at twenty-three always seems to shock people. But I've always weirdly been very traditional, which has a lot to do with growing up Jewish and going to a Modern Orthodox Jewish school. I love that so much of who I am and my values are correlated to my Jewish faith. The irony is that I'm very much a twenty-first-century girl who is also very traditional in a lot of ways. Plus, meeting and marrying my husband so young has given me the stability, time, and space to focus my energy on my career instead of on dating and bad relationships. Also, I'd be lying if I didn't mention that part of the reason I was motivated to get married so young is because I thought it would make me an eligible candidate for a role on *The Real Housewives of New York*. The joke is on me, though, because not one of the current castmates on *The Real Housewives of New York* is actually married.

As a young girl, when I envisioned my adult life, I always saw myself as a wife and a mom. I was excited about the idea of spending my life at home with my family, raising my future kids. I always wanted to be a full-time mom, maybe because I grew up with a stay-at-home mom and I loved it. I never intended to be an entrepreneur or have a business, but I just fell into it. My life now is *so* not what I had imagined it would be. I always thought I would have a kid when I was twenty-five, but now that I am twenty-six, I'm not even close to thinking about kids. But it's okay to evolve past your adolescent vision for your life, as long as you feel in control and happy with those changes. And I do, for the most part.

I sometimes feel conflicted about my change in plans. I am sad that I find myself pushing off having a family, which is something that's always been really important to me. But I love my career so much and I'm not ready to take my foot off the gas just yet. I know women, allegedly, can have it all, but at the end of the day, I'm not convinced we can. It's always going to have to be a balance of priorities.

Ben and I are fortunately on the same page in that we're

both just not ready yet. We both want to have our own big family, but for right now, there's just so much we each want to do. And that's part of the blessing of having gotten married so young. We get so many years of just being selfish, drinking and partying, and doing things that we might not be able to do with kids.

Before Ben, I had a short-lived but fabulous life as a single gal traipsing around the NYU campus. Picture Carrie Bradshaw, a few pounds heavier, listening to a lot more Taylor Swift and wearing fewer heels. Ben and I met when I was eighteen years old, so I didn't do that much damage to the New York dating scene before that. You're welcome, ladies.

It all started with my first kiss. His name was Maverick and he was fine as hell. We were in the seventh grade and I hated him. Literally, despised. He was a little bit shy but also a dick. My middle school was very small, with only about thirty kids in each grade. There were only two good-looking boys, Maverick being one of them. He had that pale complexion that turned bright red when he was embarrassed or nervous, which was cute. A big group of us were hanging out at Maverick's house one weekend when we decided to play Seven Minutes in Heaven, the classic hookup game that pairs up two kids and sends them into a dark closet for seven minutes to hopefully make out. And wouldn't you know it: I was paired up to go into the closet with Maverick.

The second we got into the closet, I was hoping we'd kiss. I had seen enough young adult movies to know that this was going to be a pivotal moment in my adolescent life. I didn't want to fuck it up. We kissed in that dark, musty closet, and I literally fell in love with him on the spot. It's true what they say: kids secretly love the kids they openly hate. That kiss opened up my floodgates. I was head over heels in love with Maverick. But back at school he continued to be a dick. Nothing had changed for him. Shockingly, he hadn't had the same change of heart that I had. At that age, boys are just not emotionally mature enough to understand the inner workings of a seventh-grade girl's mind. My secret crush was tearing me up. After school, I'd wait for him to instant-message me, but he never did.

I spent the first half of middle school hating him and the second half pining for him. I don't know if he realized I'd fallen in love with him in the closet, but I certainly wasn't up to owning my feelings back then. I just wished that he would kiss me again, but sadly, he wasn't a mind reader and continued to ignore me. Isn't that the worst thing about being thirteen or fourteen? Boys are developmentally behind and, more often than not, unable to reciprocate your feelings. You may be thinking that you've found the man of your dreams, but he doesn't even notice your new bangs. When I started to develop overwhelming feelings for boys who barely noticed me is when I really dove deep into the emo music scene. Artists like the Fray and Secondhand Serenade were singing about things that validated my intense feelings. The lyrics made me feel so seen and like I wasn't crazy for thinking about my crushes twenty-four hours a day. When Secondhand Serenade sang, "Tonight will be the night / That I will fall for you over again," I felt that in my fourteen-year-old soul.

The following year, I moved into the city and switched schools for the eighth grade. I haven't seen Maverick since then, but part of me hopes he remembers that special moment in his basement closet and maybe, just maybe, he stalks my Instagram every now and then. A girl can dream!

I've actually spoken about Maverick on the podcast a lot because he's such a formative part of my womanhood. The podcast audience is very specific, and there's no doubt in my mind that one of his female friends or his sister might have heard the podcast and told him about it. Through Jewish geography or the Northeastern summer camp network, everyone is connected. I always talk about people on the podcast, knowing that, more often than not, they're going to hear about it. Even when I called my high school English teacher "creepy" on the podcast; I got a message from him on Facebook. It was deeply uncomfortable. This is also the English teacher I fantasized about having a love affair with. When I was his student, he was an author, and he released a book about a private school in New York where a teacher had an affair with a student. It was a little too on the nose, which is why I called him "creepy" on the podcast years later and why I thought an affair was possible in the first place. Obviously, we never had the affair, but he did think my remarks were "funny."

Once I moved to the city from Long Island, the kids were more mature and there were girls who had real boyfriends and handled their emotions more like adults. Realistically, I had very little experience with boys, but I was excited to be around kids who seemed to be more on my level. My first summer after switching schools, I also switched camps. I ended up going to Camp Seneca Lake, a Jewish camp where all my new friends went, for two summers. I felt like I would have an easier time cementing my new friendships if I joined my friends at camp in the summer. And that's where I had my first boyfriend: Jordy.

We were truly the Jewish Romeo and Juliet. Jordy was from California. I lived in New York. And we spent the whole blissful summer together. Jordy was the cutest boy in camp whom everyone had a crush on. He was tall, handsome, very cool, and good at basketball. He'd been at camp for several summers and knew everyone. All the girls in my division had known Jordy for far longer, they were prettier than me, and they all crushed on him. But he liked me. I couldn't believe it. I knew I was the funniest and coolest camper, but I didn't think I was the most beautiful. But Jordy must have looked past the superficial and seen something more in me. I've always been so secure in who I am but not always in the way that I look. On a regular basis, I teeter between thinking I'm so stunning and thinking I'm heinous. So getting approval from popular boys when I was in the eighth grade was the biggest validation I could get.

Our relationship was the standard Jewish summer camp fling. On Saturdays, when the camp activities were paused for Shabbat, Jordy and I would take a Shabbat walk down to the lake and make out. Everyone would hang out by the dining hall, and the couples would take a stroll to find a secluded spot to "talk." When Jordy grabbed my hand and I sensed all eyes on me as we meandered down to the lake, I felt like Princess Diana walking down the center aisle of Westminster Abbey.

I was really devastated when the summer ended. It meant we were breaking up and heading back to our respective coasts. We kept in touch a little, but I knew things would never be the same until we got back to camp.

The following summer, Jordy and I both returned to camp. I had every intention of picking up where we'd left off, but something was different about Jordy. He seemed to have changed his mind about me. He barely even acknowledged me. He went out of his way to not see or speak to me. I couldn't figure out what had happened. I just assumed he was in his own weird, hormonal headspace, but I was let down and genuinely offended he didn't want to be my boyfriend again. Was it something I said?

My summer relationship with Jordy gave me a little street cred with my new friends at school. They saw that I had nailed down a hot boyfriend at camp, and it made people think I was cool. It gave me a little boost of confidence, even though we didn't make it as a couple. I was a girl who people knew was officially on the market.

When I got to high school, there was a different standard for how couples behaved at school given the fact that we were in a religious setting. It was a lot more reserved; no one was sucking face or dry-humping in the hallways. I wasn't prepared for this because movies, like *Never Been Kissed* and *Mean Girls*, had taught me differently. There were a few students in relationships, but they were more committed and serious. Their families knew each other. And no one was having sex. Premarital sex was a big no-no according to the Torah.

I never had something exclusive or committed in high school; I was just having fun. I was not interested in having a boyfriend. I had a friend who was dating a cool, older guy, which should've been fun for her, but they fought constantly. They both seemed kind of miserable, to be honest. I distinctly remember thinking: *Who needs that bullshit?*

I don't even think of sex as a part of my high school experience, which is so rare these days. And it had a lot to do with going to a religious school, but it also had to do with the time we were living in. Kids these days are crazy. They're posting

TikToks in skimpy bikinis and are being sexualized at a younger age. Tenth-grade me had a gap in her teeth and wore a skirt to her knees. Tenth graders today wear crop tops and have lip filler. Things are just different.

Ben and I dated seriously for most of my time at NYU. As we got closer to my college graduation, Ben and I talked more and more about getting engaged. Most girls I know are really involved in choosing their ring, and while they don't know exactly when they're going to get engaged, they have a good idea of when it's going to happen. I was hell-bent on being genuinely surprised. I told Ben not to tell me anything about the ring or the proposal. We got engaged in June, a month after I had graduated, while I was working to build Girl With No Job. At the time, I had a long-term contract with the liquor company Diageo, doing a lot of events and branded content for Don Julio, Captain Morgan, and Ketel One. After two years of working with them, I had become good friends with a lot of the people at Diageo's office and their marketing agency. It was my biggest brand partnership and I was making the most money from them of all my partners. So when one of the directors of the agency emailed me, inviting me to a shareholders' meeting to present everything I was doing on Instagram, I was honored.

The meeting was held at Lincoln Center, and Ben planned to come with me. It was an unseasonably warm June evening, and

Me and Michael Oshry, The Big O.
You can see where I got my double chin from.

ROUSE

RE

JERSEY SHORE

GTL FOR SVP!
DO YOU WANT TANNING BOOTHS IN THE
LOCKER ROOMS?
DO YOU WANT PICKLES IN THE SALAD BAR?

My ad campaign for senior vice president.
Obviously not effective.

Me, Margo, Jackie, and Olivia, Camp Pocono Trails.

Move-in day at NYU,
Weinstein Residence Hall

Freshmen orientation at
NYU, 2012. Go Violets!

My dorm room

Nu behöver man bara skaffa en dator
och börja twittra skämt – det är häftigt!

Being interviewed for *Kobra* in the back of a limousine.

My first appearance on *Steve Harvey*.
That neckline is all you need to know about what I wore.

Steve Harvey
0:22

Me and my pink skateboard. Right before I fell on my ass.

Photograph by Jason S. Abramson

The Morning Breath, Day One.

Bartending for Andy Cohen on *Watch What Happens Live.*

On the red carpet before Comedy Central's roast of Rob Lowe.
I wasn't kidding when I said I looked like a baked potato.

Say Yes to the Dress; longest day of my life.

Photograph by Olivia Oshry

Mr. and Mrs. No Job

Photograph by Anthony Vazquez

With Andy Cohen right before we smoked pot
(and before I started getting lip injections, clearly).

Photograph by Rachel Aschendorf

First comedy show at Caroline's.
Please note the McDonald's fountain soda behind me.

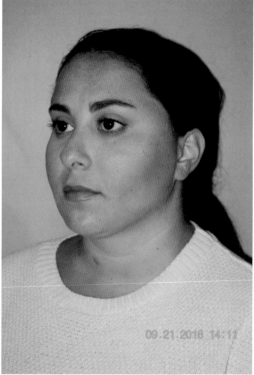

Natural neck lift (before)

Courtesy of Dr. Sharon Giese

Natural neck lift (after)

Courtesy of Dr. Sharon Giese

Cole Swindell's dressing room, Huntsville, Alabama.

Barhopping with Margo after my show in Alabama.

Yachting with the queen. Before we almost died.

Happy Halloween from me, my ex-boyfriend, his perfect wife, and friends.

The Beacon Theatre

Photograph by Anthony Vazquez

I, thanks to the heat, was having a hard time finding something to wear. Nothing looked or felt good. Don't you hate those days? I wanted to look professional and mature but nothing in my wardrobe exactly shouted "shareholders' meeting." After trying on a bunch of things, I ended up choosing a cheap black romper and chunky yellow wedges. I hated the way I looked but was running late. It was just one of those days where nothing's coming together and if you try on one more outfit you're going to need to be institutionalized. Ben was getting stressed about the timing, which was unusual because he never cares about that. I thought it was so weird that he cared so much about the time.

We rolled up to Lincoln Center, looking for the building. By the fountain there were violin players and a photographer. I remember thinking how weirdly formal it was for a shareholders' meeting. I instantly regretted my outfit choice. As I turned around to ask Ben what the fuck was going on, he got down on one knee and started crying. I don't even remember what he said because all I could see was the blue velvet jewelry box in his hand. I was so excited and genuinely surprised. I didn't even care what the ring—which, by the way, was a gorgeous princess-cut stone with a diamond band—looked like. I was ecstatic but also *slightly* let down there wasn't a real shareholders' meeting. I wanted to meet the shareholders!

Ben told me our families were across the street at the Empire Hotel waiting for us. We were going to have dinner. How fun! I love dinner! We walked one block and I was being so annoying, literally screaming, "I'm engaged!!!!!!!" to everyone who walked by. Strangers were congratulating me and being so nice to the crazy girl screaming in the street. It was very un–New York of them. Upon entering the hotel, we walked up to the restaurant, and instead of just our families, all of our friends and family were waiting in a private room to celebrate with us. I was so happy to see everyone. Seeing all the people I love in one room was the best part of the night. I got absolutely wasted.

After we got engaged in June, I didn't even think about wedding planning until the fall. I was so happy to be engaged and I wasn't ready to start thinking about it. I do wish I'd had a shorter engagement, because wedding planning is treacherous as hell and the less amount of time you have to do it, the better. As if the wedding planning process weren't stressful enough, I had landed a huge partnership with The Knot, so my wedding felt more like work than it did a party.

The dress is what I struggled with the most. I know it's most brides' favorite part of wedding planning, but I was overeating due to all the stress and had no interest in trying on dresses— let alone white ones. I had worn black to almost every single formal event for most of my life and I wasn't exactly excited to change that.

Just as I started to plan the wedding, I got an email from a producer of *Say Yes to the Dress*. I had my reservations about trying on dresses on TV, but I thought it would be a great way to find a dress *and* promote my brand. Two birds, one stone type of thing. I ended up negotiating a great deal with Kleinfeld in exchange for doing the episode. They would give me a $10,000 credit in exchange for my promoting the episode on my Instagram. As dreamy as that sounds, the idea alone of trying on wedding dresses made me want to cry. But trying on dresses on *national television* made me want to die.

It was not what I expected. I don't regret doing it because oddly enough, to this day, so many people come up to me and recognize me from *Say Yes to the Dress*. It opened me up to an entirely new demographic. Years after the episode aired, I was in a corporate office building, getting a soda from the vending machine (obviously), when an older receptionist came up to me and recognized me from the show. She said she and her daughter loved the episode, and it made me feel so good. So it was good exposure and supposed to be a fun outing, but the day itself was . . . hard.

Trying on wedding dresses in any circumstance is hard work. The dresses are heavy. It's exhausting and you're a little sweaty the whole time. If you have a body like mine, you're also in a full Spanx getup, which adds to the heat and discomfort. I felt like a sweaty sausage trying to fit into those dresses. Plus, I had to deal with producers of the show who didn't really care if I was feeling insecure. It was not a good look for me. The bright fluorescent lights, the long day of film-ing, and the physical effort of taking on and off thirty pounds of lace, tulle, and taffeta wasn't adding up to the glowy bridal look of my dreams.

At the end of the episode, there was a dress that I kind of liked, but I wasn't ready to make a real-life decision at that mo-ment. The producers told me I didn't need to choose a dress in real life but asked if I'd just pick one for the show. They wanted me to actually say yes to the dress for the show. I understand how television works and I did actually like the dress, so I hap-pily agreed. I said I was going to come back to Kleinfeld off camera and choose my dress for real. When I did go back to the store, I tried to take another look at that dress, but it was gone. That's the question I get asked the most from people when they see pictures from my wedding. They think I'm some sort of fraud for not wearing the dress from the show, and they're not wrong.

When the episode finally aired, I wasn't thrilled with how I came off. There are two brides featured per episode, but you don't know the other bride's story and experiences until it airs. My story and requirements were that I wanted long sleeves for my traditional Orthodox Jewish wedding. The editing of the episode made it seem like I was so unreasonable for wanting a long-sleeve dress. It was as if I'd come in asking for a black snakeskin wedding dress. The consultant helping me was running around the store yelling, "Long sleeve! Long sleeve!" like her hair was on fire.

The real kicker was the other bride featured on my episode. She was from Louisiana and had lost her entire house, including her wedding dress, in a flood. Randy went to Louisiana on behalf of Kleinfeld, where they ended up paying for her entire wedding. It was an emotional episode; I even found myself getting choked up toward the end. So they're cutting between this poor, sweet girl in Louisiana who lost her whole wedding, and me, the big annoying JAP complaining about her long-sleeve dress. It was such an intentional juxtaposition. As soon as I saw the episode, I just knew people were going to paint me as this spoiled brat. I've been called worse, no doubt. But it was my first experience calling bullshit on TV and feeling naive for assuming I would be portrayed in the exact light I wanted to be.

When I later found out the original dress from the show was no longer available, I tried on a bunch of dresses at Kleinfeld and found a dress that I kind of liked. I needed to add the long sleeves and a few other customizations. The dress designer was in Italy but agreed to make me a custom gown completely free. With absolutely no knowledge of how to customize a gown, I customized a gown. I changed pretty much everything about the original dress. It took nine months to make, and I finally got to try it on for the first time in July before my September wedding. The designer came in from Italy for my first fitting. It should've been an honor, but the moment I saw the dress I started sobbing. It was heinous and did nothing for my body. I mean, I don't know anything about fashion. Who the fuck did I think I was, designing a dress? It was so awkward because I truly didn't want to offend the designer. My family intervened and defused the situation. They suggested we take a break and get something to eat (they know me so well). I never went back to Kleinfeld to get my free dress. I ended up getting a dress that I loved (and did not design) off the rack from Oleg Cassini at David's Bridal. It wasn't the custom Italian gown I'd dreamed of, but it was beautiful, and more important, it fit like a glove.

When it came to planning the details of the wedding and reception, I didn't care what anyone wanted. It was my day, nobody else's. Not even Ben's. I chose everything. Ben got to choose the song he danced to with his mom, which was so generous of me. We got married in a landmark synagogue on the Lower East Side.

To me, the reception was much less important than the wedding ceremony itself. I was much more deliberate in choosing meaningful details for our ceremony. For the chuppah (the canopy over the altar where the bride and groom stand for the ceremony), we used my dad's tallit (prayer shawl), and it meant the world to me to include him and honor him on this big day. We had an amazing Jewish boys' choir, comprised of six ten-year-old kids, who sang me down the aisle. It was so powerful. In traditional Jewish weddings, unlike the many Christian or nondenominational ceremonies you see in movies, the bride and groom don't recite vows. But I asked the rabbi if Ben and I could say something to each other because I just wanted to make it feel personal and special to us. And it really was.

I really feel like I had two weddings. The first was the ceremony, which is where I put most of my effort in making it intimate. There was a no-phone rule, so everyone could be really present in the moment with us. I didn't care about the Instagram-ability. I wanted it to be serious. We focused on our faith and our families.

But with the reception, I was so shallow about the whole thing. I thought of the reception with the mindset of how it would look in pictures and on Instagram. The Knot was covering my wedding as part of our collaboration, and they wanted the exclusive photos. I thought of the entire wedding as a branded event with various sponsors and business relationships involved, not as a life moment. That decision isn't for everyone, and it came with a few compromises and regrets. But I held on to the ceremony as a sacred moment, and Mama got us a $400,000 wedding for much, much less.

I firmly believe that every person you date comes into your life for a reason, even if you don't realize it at the time. It's a weird metaphor, but in the Torah, there's the concept of the *malach Hashem*, which is an angel from God. They are sent out by God to pick something up and bring it to another place. I always feel like certain boys are *malach Hashem*s. They pick you up and bring you to another place in your life, teach you a lesson, or give you an experience that you needed in order to meet the next person. In this way, everyone serves a purpose, and at the end of the day, you really do learn a lesson from every person you're with, whether it's about yourself or about dating in general. So no one and no relationship is a waste of time. Whether it's in your career or in your dating life, it puts you in a different place.

If I am being honest, I would take all of my dating and wedding advice with a grain of salt. I've been on one date in my entire life. I coerced my husband into loving me. I sold my wedding to sponsors for a branded event. I've only had sex with one man. What the hell do I know? Everyone's journey is different and that's okay. As long as you're with someone who makes you laugh and feel good about yourself, what else matters?

CHAPTER FIVE

Chubby, Stubby, and Fabulous!

The most complicated relationship in my life is surprisingly not the one with my husband, my sisters, or my friends. It's the one I have with my body. My own personal experience with body image is a long, winding road filled with highs and lows, because I am not totally sure how I feel about my body. I am sure of what random strangers on the Internet think of my body, that's for sure. But when it comes to the way I see myself, I am not entirely sure what I see.

It's okay to have mixed feelings when it comes to your body and how you look. At any given moment I feel both confident and powerful, *and* like I want to slice open my inner thighs and drain them of their fat, just so I can know what it feels like to have a thigh gap. It dawned on me a few years ago that I may never have a thigh gap and that I have to be okay with that.

I am both the most *and* least confident person in the world. When I walk into a party, I feel like the most beautiful *and* the ugliest woman in the room. It's strange. I feel like I'm the best-dressed, most beautiful person, but then part of me knows in the back of my head that I'm actually like the ugliest. I know that I am lying to myself. I'm so confident in myself but that's because my confidence is something I've developed and worked to feel. But somewhere in the back of my mind, underneath all the confidence, I know that it's not genuine. Being confident is a choice, so the logical part of my brain knows that I chose to be confident. I know the reality of what I look like.

I often get asked, "How are you so confident?" in interviews, meet-and-greets, and Q & As. I get asked so frequently it makes me question why it should come as such a shock to people. Nobody is asking Gigi Hadid how she is so confident. It's as if they know that my confidence is a façade—and they're questioning it.

Confidence is a tricky bitch because everyone wants her but very few can find her. My motto when it comes to confidence is just to fake it till you make it. I came to this conclusion when I was very young, sitting on the toilet in the guest bathroom of our house. The entire bathroom was mirrored—the walls, the ceiling, the fixtures, etc. It was a frightening place to be in, let alone shit in. I remember looking at myself, particularly the mole I had on my neck that I hated (she's since been removed), and wondering how anyone was ever going to think I was pretty. I didn't even think I was pretty. In that moment I realized that if I acted like I was the most beautiful woman in the world, others might start to think that too. Or at least they'd admire my confidence. And that's exactly how I started to act. Soon enough, the way I pretended to feel about myself quickly turned into how I genuinely felt about myself.

I subscribe to the tankini philosophy of body image. When it comes to how we feel about our bodies, we're all somewhere in between. Not quite a bikini, not quite a one-piece. We suck it in and work our angles for a skinny arm in photos, while also trying to own our skin as is. You can get Botox and love yourself. You can Facetune a double chin or Photoshop a muffin top without self-loathing. We can have it all.

Have you ever heard the classic dieter phrases? You know, the ones your mom used to whisper to you as you went for your third serving of macaroni and cheese? They're meant to be inspirational but somehow always end up coming off insulting.

"Moment on the lips, forever on the hips."
"Nothing tastes as good as skinny feels."

There they are. The classics. And they're kind of true, except for when they're not. Sometimes when I'm mindlessly eating

Baked Lay's because things are getting real tense on *Vanderpump Rules*, I can see how those phrases might be helpful. But when I'm digging into a creamy penne alla vodka from Serafina, nothing in the world feels as good as that pasta tastes. So after years of painstaking research, I am here to tell you that there are, in fact, things that taste as good as skinny feels. Here are just a few:

★ Glazed donuts from Krispy Kreme
★ Chicken sandwiches from Whataburger
★ Black-and-white milkshakes from any NYC diner
★ Macaroni and cheese from Boston Market
★ Carvel ice-cream cakes
★ Anything from McDonald's (tastes better after two a.m.)
★ My mom's apple pie
★ My mother-in-law's spaghetti Bolognese

I was never made aware of my weight as a good or a bad thing. I was a very thin kid, sometimes too thin (can you imagine?). "Diet" wasn't a word I was familiar with. I thought of food strictly as fuel. I ate to live, to have the energy to do what I wanted to do. I was constantly being given extra food at meals and snacks throughout the day because my parents were worried that I was too skinny. I was too young to appreciate the compliment. It's been over a decade since someone told me I was too skinny.

My older sister Olivia wasn't as blessed. She struggled with her weight constantly, therefore making food and health common topics of conversation in our house. I was being reprimanded about my short temper; Olivia was being reprimanded about her calorie intake. We all had our own problems. While I was being told to eat more, Olivia's food intake was being closely monitored. Her weight fluctuation was a common dinner-table conversation topic, but being the skinny bitch that I was, I was mostly left out of those conversations, seeing as how I was incapable of gaining weight. I can't believe how much I have changed.

We spent our preteen summers at Camp Vega, an all-girls sleepaway camp in Fayette, Maine. It was paradise for a spoiled brat like me, and I loved every minute of it. We'd make s'mores, bake cookies, and even throw the occasional "barf party," where we'd wake up in the middle of the night to find our entire bunk floor covered in candy. The premise of the barf parties was to eat so much candy that you inevitably barfed before going back to bed. Given the fact that most of the camp activities revolved around eating—ice-cream socials, cooking classes, cookouts— it should come as a surprise to no one that Olivia gained roughly twenty pounds each summer she spent there. That was the end of Camp Vega for Olivia. My parents were worried that if Olivia returned the following summer, there'd be a shortage of food and the rest of the campers would go hungry. So in the summer of 2006, my parents decided that Olivia might benefit from spending two months at Camp Pocono Trails, a "weight loss" camp in Pennsylvania. And since we were *that* kind of family, my sisters and I were all forced to go with her. I was devastated. I loved Camp Vega and I'd miss my camp friends terribly, but family is family. So we got ourselves ready for fat camp. We watched *Heavyweights* and packed our bags. We were headed for the Poconos. Rather than tell our friends back home where we were actually going, we opted to tell them we were spending our summer at a "sports camp."

It came as a shock to everyone when we all ended up falling in love with fat camp. We chose to never return to Camp Vega. I wasn't in the weight-loss program; I was just there to support my sister. So for me it was a regular camp with regular activities. I didn't understand what was different about fat camp. Why was this camp different from all other camps?

I was twelve that first summer at fat camp. I'd just wrapped up the sixth grade and was ready to spend two months at fat camp. Sorry, "weight loss" camp. The camp itinerary was very similar to a regular camp's, except that the early morning activity involved some sort of exercise. The female campers were able to choose between step aerobics, Zumba, and boot camp. Then all the other camp activities were exactly what you'd expect at a summer camp: swimming, arts and crafts, and sports. The only difference was that when we had volleyball on our schedule, we had to actually, you know, *play* volleyball. Groundbreaking.

The most glaring differences between standard camp and fat camp were the food and the weekly weigh-ins. There were two different meal programs offered: maintenance and weight loss. I was on a maintenance program because I wasn't actually there to lose weight, so the weekly weigh-ins were optional for me. I spent my Sundays making friendship bracelets and swimming in the lake while my fellow campers lined up in the rec hall to get weighed in. There were a lot of different kids at the camp who were there for other reasons, not necessarily to lose weight. Some of them struggled with eating disorders. Those of us on maintenance received a coveted neon-yellow bracelet (my first experience with a VIP wristband), which meant we could have seconds at meals and generally do our own thing during activities. The bracelet made you special. You were now in a different class of campers, an elite one. The food offerings were fairly typical camp fare, though meals were portioned out and more healthfully prepared.

I remember fat camp feeling so normal from the moment I got there. I didn't feel different from my bunkmates, even though I was the only one not there to lose weight (I know, I can't believe it either). All of that changed for me when we took a field trip to a local water park. This was before catching coronavirus was a major concern, so I was fucking jazzed to get out there and swim in what I assumed to be the urine-filled wave pool. The camp had very, very strict policies pertaining to food on field trips. We were instructed to enjoy the park with our group and eat nothing. Looking back now, as a fat person, it was kind of a torturous activity. Water parks are famous for their snacks—funnel cake, fried Oreos, Dippin' Dots. Asking a bunch of chubby kids not to eat at a water park is like asking teenage Lindsay Lohan not to do cocaine at a rave. Cruel.

As a natural-born rebel, especially when it comes to forbidden food, I just had to buy myself a snack. A souvenir, if you will. My friend Hailey and I asked our counselor if we could go to the bathroom. With her approval, we quickly bought a giant cookie and split it in the bathroom. We looked at each other with deep satisfaction as we shoved the double-chocolate-chip cookie down our throats. We knew what we were doing was wrong, but it felt so right.

It turns out a little bitch named Morgan ratted us out to our group leader on the bus ride home from Camelbeach. I'm not sure how she knew about our bathroom fiesta but I couldn't believe she would turn us in. It was such a betrayal from our fellow camper. We were all supposed to be on the same side, Morgan. Traitor.

Back at camp, we hadn't taken two steps off the bus before we were called into our group leader's office. She started yelling and screaming, and about thirty seconds in, I realized she was only looking at Hailey. She barely even looked at me.

Hailey got in serious trouble and I basically got a slap on the wrist. Her punishment was a week of ETR and ETB—Early to Rise and Early to Bed. This meant, for a week, Hailey had to wake up an hour early and pick up trash on the lawn and then go straight to bed after dinner. I walked out of the office with one night of ETB.

That was the first time I realized there was a difference between Hailey and me. We were being treated differently for one reason: she was fat and I was skinny. This was the first of many times in my life where I would be treated differently simply because of my weight. It was in that moment, in my group leader's office, that I learned a valuable lesson—skinny people can do whatever the fuck they want. The rules are different for them. When Rihanna wears assless chaps to an NBA game, it's cool and sexy. When Lizzo does, it's vulgar and inappropriate for children to see. See what I am getting at?

Fat camp was full of firsts for me. I put in my first tampon in bunk I3; I sharted for the first time in bunk H5. It was magical! The shart wasn't my finest moment, obviously. I didn't know you could shit and fart at the same time. It was all very new to me. I had made a critical error earlier that day during snack time. Once a week, our midday snack was an off-brand "Fudgsicle," and while it was delicious, it was also dangerous. The "Fudgsicles" were sugar free and included a little ingredient called sorbitol—a sugar alternative that can lead to abdominal pain, flatulence, and mild-to-severe diarrhea if ingested in large amounts. Being that I could have as many snacks as I wanted, I went for two "Fudgsicles" on that particularly sunny Saturday. Do I really need to tell you what happened next?

While fat camp was a wonderful experience filled with wonderful memories, like shitting my pants, I think that it may have impacted my mental health more than I realized. Now, I don't know if I'm just blaming my struggle with weight on the experience of going to fat camp, but I do remember seeing how food became something people coveted. Even though I wasn't technically deprived at camp, I couldn't shake this anxiety that every meal could be my last. If you've ever seen me eat, you know I still haven't shaken this feeling. It's like someone is timing me.

Fat camp was the first time I was ever in the presence of girls my age who had complicated relationships with eating, and I think being around it at a young age when I was particularly impressionable was toxic. Because I picked up on the way that some of the other campers looked at their own bodies or were critical of themselves. It was shocking for me to be around girls my age who had so much to say about the way that they looked. I don't know if I would necessarily still have struggled with my weight later anyway, but it was a very eye-opening experience.

Since my time at fat camp, my weight has followed me, consuming my innermost thoughts and insecurities. She's a stage-five clinger and I can't seem to get away from her. When I was in high school, I considered myself the fat friend. I had such a complex about my body at the time, constantly comparing myself to my friends and making jokes about my double chin. When we'd take trips for spring break, I would always wear a tankini—an interesting choice for a fifteen-year-old but one I felt was necessary. Tankinis covered up my belly, always a problem area for me, while still looking stylish and cute. And by "cute," I mean appropriate for a middle-aged soccer mom from Connecticut. I don't know why I thought I was so fat, but I always considered myself the token fat friend. When I look back at pictures from high school, I look just like everyone else. I certainly wasn't fat. It makes me sad to think of all the time I spent feeling insecure about my body when I never had anything to be insecure about.

My metabolism did eventually catch up with me when I got to college. I mean, don't get me wrong; I still have a very fast metabolism. Given what I eat in a day, I should be featured on *My 600-lb Life*. But that first year at camp was when I realized that food wasn't just food. It was this complicated thing. It could be an addiction.

Being in the fat camp environment certainly had a profound effect on my relationship with my body. But more than anything, working in and being a huge fan of pop culture has made me question how I see myself. The standard of beauty has changed in recent years. All the people who are successful and famous aren't exclusively size zeros anymore. Thank God for that, because if I had been born fifteen years earlier and still looked the way I do now, I may not have become the sex symbol I am today.

I know that not many would consider them the greatest role models for everything, but I actually really love and relate to the Kardashians on most things, and this topic in particular. They've always been very open and honest on their show about their struggles with weight and the effort they put into looking their best. I respect how open they are about the struggle, and as someone who has been struggling since she was a teenager, I feel so seen by them. They're transparent about how much they work out, their struggles with losing weight, and how it all affects them mentally and emotionally. Khloe and Kim in particular. I feel the same way. They're even (semi) open about the work they get done. It's very cool to see huge celebrities having the same relationship with body image and food as I do.

Celebrities tend to just show up on red carpets looking amazing, trying to make fans believe that this is how they were born. I like knowing that Kim Kardashian works really fucking hard to look that snatched. That makes me feel good, because I'm not working hard, and that's why I don't look like her. There's nothing wrong with me! They are so much more authentic to me than every model taking a photo "eating" a slice of pizza.

Spoiler alert—that's not the body of someone who eats pizza. I'll show you what the body of someone who eats pizza regularly looks like, and believe me, it's not that.

There is a growing number of actresses, singers, and public figures who don't cave in to the long-established industry pressures to look a particular (thin) way. I love these people because I am one of them. Throughout the eight years I've been working in the public eye, I have never lost weight solely for the approval of others, and I am proud of that, because there were times when I read what people were saying about me online or I saw a photo of myself that made me want to run to the nearest Weight Watchers meeting. Having strangers comment on your body, when you never asked them to, is a very strange, invasive feeling—one that you have to grow accustomed to if you choose to live a public life.

I've always felt some sort of responsibility to my audience to be real when it comes to my weight. TV and movies are constantly portraying fat people as lazy pieces of shit. There's a misconception that you can't start living a happy and full life until you reach your goal weight, but here I am debunking that. I have a husband who loves me, a family that tolerates me, a boppin' career, *and* a FUPA. I was wrong earlier: you truly can have it all!

Now that we're on the subject of FUPAs, can we quickly discuss how fucking infuriating they are? A FUPA—for those who don't know—is the area above your vagina or penis where fat tends to congregate. "FUPA" stands for "Fat Upper Pubic Area," but I call it the Fat Upper Pussy Area. Different strokes for different folks.

My FUPA is my archnemesis. She is always showing up places uninvited. She shows up under blouses, pants, and even poufy dresses. No matter how much my weight fluctuates, you can always count on my Fat Upper Pussy Area to be alive and well.

Still, though, there's an underlying expectation of what to look like if you want to be successful. Deep down I know that if I'd always been thin, my life would be very different right now. Doors would open a little more easily, and if nothing else, I would feel more comfortable in my own skin as I promote myself and my brand. I'd be shaking my titties in a bikini because I know that's what sells. When I post photos showing more skin or appearing to look thinner than usual, they usually, if not always, outperform photos where I don't. There's an underlying expectation of what you should look like in order to be successful, especially in Hollywood, and there's always some sense that you've made it against the odds if you dare to be chubby.

I have this theory that when you're a fat person living in a skinny person's world, you have to try harder. You're held to a higher standard. You have to be funnier and more likable because you have to prove to everyone that you deserve to be there. Just based on the way you look, people will think that you don't deserve success. It's so fucked up to say out loud, but I don't think I would be half the comedian I am if I had never encountered situations where people were making fun of my weight. That kind of humiliation gives you resilience, but more important, it gives you this never-ending thirst for people's approval. You want people to think they were wrong about you— because they were.

Being fat is a personality trait that no one can understand unless they've been fat before. When you are fat, you have to be the funniest or smartest person in every room in order to prove why you're in that room in the first place. For me, I've tended to use humor as a defense mechanism to deflect the possibility of anyone calling me fat. Because if you call yourself fat first, nobody else will. We're only on chapter 5 and I must have referred to myself as "chubby" at least five times by now. I choose to be funny to prevent people from noticing my weight. It's paranoia—that I'm different, fatter than my friends. I combat my paranoia and insecurity by being funny.

I like to joke about my weight because it's relatable and it makes us all feel better about our own internal bullshit. In one way or another, everyone has struggled with looking in the mirror and not being overjoyed at what they see looking back. You show me someone who says they have no insecurities, and I'll show you a liar.

Worrying about your weight affects so many facets of your life because you're thinking about it all the time—or at least I am. I'm always thinking about what I'm eating and how I look. When I land a big work opportunity, I'm 50 percent excited and 50 percent hoping it gets cancelled because then I won't have to find something to wear. It affects more aspects of my life than I even realize. You know those friends who don't think about food or dieting at all? They're just *living*. Those people who can walk up a flight of stairs while having a full-on conversation and not get out of breath. Those people who are blissfully unaware of the judgment surrounding bowls of candy in their office. The people who don't hate beautiful spring days because they don't remind them that the dreaded swimsuit season is around the corner. I'm so jealous of those people. I hate those people.

My life is the exact opposite. I am constantly hungry. I am constantly planning out my next meal. I am constantly worried about getting out of breath onstage. I am constantly tugging at my blouse to make sure it covers my stomach properly. I am constantly getting teary-eyed in department store dressing rooms. I am constantly stretching out my clothes before I put them on. Being fat is exhausting not only physically but mentally.

I invest a lot in being funny and being personable because it compensates for my being chubby. And being funny has gotten me far. While some girls get invited places because they're hot, people will say, "Let's invite Claudia to the party. She's so much fun!" I'll spend more time on my hair and makeup than I probably would otherwise because I actually can control that, unlike my weight. Skinny people can just roll out of bed and still look pretty. I can't. They throw on a T-shirt, show off their delicate collarbones, and put on some ChapStick. What's that like?

Chubby people shoulder an additional burden of worry about their bodies that affects so many parts of their lives. Because fat people are an unprotected group, really, and not considered a minority or a marginalized group. Fat people are the last frontier of people that it's still okay to make fun of. I watch so much *RuPaul's Drag Race* and I love it. Part of what I love is how everyone is always poking fun at each other while maintaining a hard line about things that are off-limits. They're sensitive to each other's struggles while they're being bitchy. Being fat is not one of those protected sensitivities. Weight is the first thing they come at each other for. It's an unprotected characteristic, unlike so many others, and they apparently have no qualms about going for the (chubby) jugular.

Shopping can be a minefield of emotions when you aren't a size two. Most clothing isn't designed for people who look like me, people with FUPAs and fat asses. It's certainly not designed for people with 36G-sized breasts. I absolutely loathe the process of shopping because I always end up frustrated, sweating, and more in my own head than ever. Of course, I want to look cute and snatched—who doesn't?—and I finally have the money to buy nice things, but they usually don't come in my size or fit me well. We all feel a certain pressure to have nice things, especially when you're in the public eye, but I'm very limited by my body. I choose to invest in designer bags, shoes, and jewelry, which work for me at any size. Chanel bags are one-size-fits-all and I LIVE BY THAT.

My insecurities and areas where I fall flat are constantly top of mind for me, and I am actively trying to not let them take over my life. Regardless of my weight, I have always tried to love myself and be happy with who I am. That sounds like an after-school special, but it's true. I've always had a healthy sense of self-confidence, even if it was a façade, because my weight never affected my ability to have a full life. Having said that, becoming a more well-known public person puts all your deepest insecurities on a platter for the world to feast on. Becoming a public figure made me care more about my weight than ever before, and I hate that. When I see myself on TV or in photographs, it's hard not to look critically and wish that I hadn't eaten two donuts before the interview.

I try to be totally neutral when it comes to my body and how I see myself, but that's virtually impossible. Every now and then, I'll see a photo or video that'll leave me shooketh. I *think* I have a good idea of what I look like, but it's possible that my perception of my body is far from reality.

Those thoughts always leave me at a crossroads. I feel depressed about my body, but I'm too lazy to work out and I'm too hungry to stop eating. So what's a girl to do? I refuse to take any action. The last (and first official) time I went on a true diet was in June 2018, right after I got my chin procedure done. I had hated my double chin for so long. I'd been told my whole life to embrace my insecurities, and I tried, but my double chin was something I just couldn't get on board with. Unlike my FUPA, I couldn't hide my double chin with an oversized T-shirt. My double chin showed up in photos, at events, and even in my strategically angled Instagram stories. I couldn't hide it, and that killed me the most. One day, this light went off in my head and I thought, *Why the fuck do I have to embrace my insecurities? Because some quote card on Instagram is telling me to? Why can't I change something that bothers me?* So I did. I left my second chin on an operating table on Park Avenue, said my goodbyes, and never looked back.

The decision to get the chin procedure took me all of two seconds to make. I had been dying to get Kybella injections in my neck/jawline to shrink my double chin ever since I saw Brittany Cartwright from *Vanderpump Rules* talk about it in *People* magazine. I had never had any cosmetic procedures done before, nor had I ever been to a plastic surgeon, so I had no clue where to start. My sister Jackie and I had been talking about how good Ramona Singer looked on the *Real Housewives of New York City* reunion that week and decided that whoever was working on Ramona's face needed to work on mine, too. Only the best for me and the Ramonacoaster!

Thanks to Google, I ended up at Dr. Sharon Giese's office one week later. Much to my chagrin, she said she really didn't recommend Kybella since it only had a 50 percent success rate and was very, very painful. Instead she suggested a procedure that she called the Natural Neck Lift, which is essentially out-patient liposuction. I didn't think twice about getting it done. It was the solution to all my problems. Plus, all of my sisters thought it was a good idea, and whatever they say, I do.

Ben was, as always, supportive of my decision, but he also felt the need to stress that I was naturally beautiful and I didn't need to get anything done to my face. It was very sweet but I told him to kindly shut the fuck up. I had already made up my mind. Love may be blind, but I'm not.

I felt sure of my decision because I was doing it completely for myself. And if you're going to do this type of thing, it has to be because it's what *you* want to do. It's always nice to have the support of your friends and family, but at the end of the day it isn't for them. Ben's opinion is important to me in general, and in matters like this, he's entitled to his opinion, but it's my body and I am going to make the final decision. When I want to get Botox or filler, I tell him about it and we have an in-depth discussion about the potential risks and outcomes.

But when Ben gets a haircut, we don't have a whole meeting about it. I smell a double standard!

Regardless, Ben is mostly useless when it comes to giving me feedback on my appearance. If I ask him about an outfit I'm wearing, he just tells me I look great, when I usually don't. I understand that I tricked him into falling in love with me all those years ago and he's been under a spell ever since, but sometimes I just need an honest opinion, even if it means he's telling me I look fat in these jeans.

The procedure itself took about forty-five minutes. Dr. Giese inserted a little needle behind my earlobe and sucked out all excess fat from my jowls, neck, and cheeks. There was no general anesthesia involved, which I was relieved about. I've had a phobia of anesthetic ever since seeing a terrifying episode of *Nip/Tuck* where a patient had an adverse reaction to anesthesia and was awake but paralyzed for her entire procedure. Instead, Dr. Giese just used localized numbing and gave me a mighty big Valium.

I don't remember much about the procedure but my sister Olivia was in the waiting room and she said you could hear me screaming before you walked through the front door. I have a very low tolerance for pain, did I not mention that? Since I was awake and somewhat cognizant of what was happening during the procedure, I could hear the clanging of the tools and, even worse, the sound of my skin being lifted. That freaked me out and was most likely the cause of my screaming. The second I got home from the procedure, I couldn't wait to rip the bandages off and see the results.

The full recovery process took three months in terms of all the swelling going down and being able to see the final results. I woke up every day and took pictures of my neck, documenting the healing process. I have thousands of photos on my camera roll of my chin at different angles and various stages of bruising. On my final post-op visit to Dr. Giese, she showed me the official before-and-after pictures. I was floored. And I obviously couldn't wait to post them on Instagram.

I was a little nervous to post, not for fear of judgment or ridicule, but because I hated the way I looked in the before shot. The before was *sooooo* before. But I've always been open and honest with my audience and my chin was no exception. I didn't sign up for this life to do it half-assed, so I posted the photos with no regrets.

I figured if I wanted the best chance at looking snatched after the surgery, I should set myself up for success and stop eating crap once and for all. Since I refused to work out, I knew if I wanted to lose any weight I would actually have to stop eating shit. I dieted for the rest of the year, a good six months. It was brutal. I traded in my chicken nuggets for grilled chicken to give myself the best possible chance once the results of the surgery were done. While I loathed being on a diet, I was enjoying my newfound relationship with alcohol. Because I was no longer loading up on carbs, I was three sheets to the wind after two margaritas. It used to take five or six drinks to get me drunk, but being on a diet had its perks.

Another perk was all the time I had on my hands. I was no longer worrying about choosing a shirt that hid my FUPA or a dress that didn't show my girdle. I wasn't constantly pulling on my dress or adjusting my Spanx at parties. I was having a lot more fun. It was eye-opening. I felt so much less aware of my body. I was living in the moment, enjoying myself without the mental toll that it takes to be constantly thinking about your body.

The diet lasted six months. I started to feel happy in my own skin and decided that I didn't want to continue losing weight. I like having a little meat on my bones, and so much of who I am/my comedy is about my weight; I didn't want to become unrelatable.

Ever since my foray into plastic surgery, I have been getting Botox twice a year and lip filler once a year. I enjoy doing the Botox because I genuinely believe that it is preventative. I have a few developing wrinkles on my forehead that, if I take care of them now, will never become an issue. I like to think sixty-year-old me will be grateful to twenty-five-year-old me for being responsible. But I have a weird relationship with my lip filler. I did it once kind of as an experiment, just to see what I would look like. I did a very little amount, so it still looked natural. And I liked the results. Then I did it again and I went bigger. I remember feeling really stupid afterward. My lips had never been something that bothered me, so I didn't understand why I was actively trying to change them. I still get the filler once a year, though. I just think it's cool to say: "I get lip filler." It might be the shallowest thing about me. I'm easily influenced by what I see on TV or online, and these days if you don't have filler in your lips, you're not going to make it very far. So even though I don't think I need it, I still go in once a year to get it done. I like telling people I get my lips done; I feel like it gives me clout. How sad is that?

I remember watching an episode of *Vanderpump Rules* where Scheana and Kristen went to the doctor's office for Botox. These beautiful young girls, in the prime of their lives, were getting a treatment I thought was for old people. I didn't get it. They were at the doctor's office explaining how it's totally preventative and that they've been doing it since they were twenty-five. It was a really eye-opening moment that influenced my decision to have it done. And to answer your question, yes, I take most of my beauty and medical advice from the *Vanderpump Rules* gang. Who else?

I plan to age gracefully. I'm not afraid of aging, but I would like to age a little more gracefully than others. I mean, we live in a youth-obsessed culture where teenagers are being paid

$250,000 to record videos of themselves dancing in a crop top. How can I not be getting Botox? No one over the age of twenty-one can keep up. I'm twenty-six and I'm considered a grandmother in the digital community.

Being yourself, whether you're a hundred pounds or four hundred pounds, is an incredibly brave thing to do. People on the Internet can be evil, and I respect anyone who puts themselves out there, publicly, with confidence. My advice to all of you when it comes to confidence is to go under the knife. No, I'm just kidding. But I do believe that if there's something really bothering you and you just can't accept it, you should do something about it. As they say in Alcoholics Anonymous:

> God, grant me the serenity to accept the things I cannot change, the courage to change the things I can, and the wisdom to know the difference.

I mean, I've never been to an AA meeting, but it's definitely in my future.

CHAPTER SIX

Will All the Real Stans Please Stand Up?

I t's never been a better time to be a fan. We have unparalleled access to our favorite musicians, actors, and reality stars, thanks largely to social media. There's a new sense of intimacy and connection. At the click of a button, Shawn Mendes can share what color underwear he is wearing and what he and Camila Cabello ate for lunch that day. As idols and icons tweet, Instagram, and Tok about their formerly private lives, they're giving us a direct line into their most intimate moments. As a professional fan myself, it's a dream. I'm so glad

I am alive now, because being a fan has never been more fun and interactive than it is today.

This new, intimate access to our favorite celebrities has created the great marvel of "standom," where fans feel a deeply personal, passionate, borderline-obsessive connection. Stans make the brave choice and go to great lengths to defend their idols in the face of scandal, error, or artistic misfire. The term "stan" was coined by Eminem—the rapper, not the candy.

Die-hard fan bases have created their own identities and communities, largely online, with monikers as badges of honor. Beliebers. Little Monsters. Swifties. Beyhive. Toasters (my favorite ones). Teens are often at the heart of intense fandoms and stan culture, because who has more time than them to engage in the never-ending online rhetoric of celebrity culture? Their raging hormones and proclivity for drama make them the perfect people to dive into true standom.

I had the great privilege of growing up in the age of boy bands. *NSYNC and Backstreet Boys created a great debate among my generation and in my house. The bubblegum sounds and overly gelled hair of boy bands were the fabric of my formative years. For the Oshry sisters of Long Island, the debate between *NSYNC and Backstreet Boys created a sisterhood divided. It was a war as intense as that of Coke vs. Pepsi. You identified as either a Justin Timberlake girl or a Nick Carter girl. You couldn't be both.

I didn't really understand the magnitude of such an allegiance at the time, but Olivia and Jackie were as die-hard as you could get back then. Olivia firmly believed in the unparalleled talents of JC Chasez. Her school supplies were official *NSYNC merchandise, a full set of the coordinating folders, notebooks, and pencil cases. If you wanted to hang out in Olivia's room and gain access to her desktop computer, as adolescent Claudia always did, you had to pledge your allegiance to *NSYNC. Olivia had a life-sized poster of *NSYNC above her bed so JC and Justin Timberlake could tuck her in at night and watch her sleep. Jackie's room had the same poster, from the same company, but of Backstreet Boys. This is where things got complicated.

Since Margo and I were younger and less certain of which side to choose, they each campaigned for us to join them. As kids we often slept in each other's beds. If I wanted to bunk with Olivia, I'd have to join her in hyping up the achievements of *NSYNC. She'd keep you up after bedtime proselytizing as to why *NSYNC was superior. She would try to explain to me why Nick Carter was a fraud and how important it was that I agree with her. While Jackie was maybe less of a militant promoter, she'd try to convert us to Backstreet Boys by offering us a peek into her normally private bedroom, which was by far the biggest in the house. She had a big TV, too, which was a huge draw for young Claudia.

While this was my first observation of real fandom, it was more their thing than it was mine. Margo and I just tried to use it to our advantage if we wanted to hang out in one of their rooms or use their computers to download music illegally.

For me, true standom came by way of the Disney Channel, and specifically those three fine-ass brothers from Wyckoff, New Jersey. In the summer of 2008, when I was thirteen and ready to dive into a life of passionate fan responsibilities, the Jonas Brothers starred in the Disney Channel original movie (or as we called it, DCOM) *Camp Rock* and in 2010 its sequel, *Camp Rock 2: The Final Jam.* These were pivotal films for me. Between Joe Jonas and the celebration of camp, it was a culmination of all the things I loved.

Part of being a true Jonas Brothers fan was picking your favorite brother. For me, it was undeniably Joe. He had the charisma, uniqueness, nerve, and talent to take over the world. But the fandom was divided when it came to picking a favorite. Nick was younger, was arguably more musically talented, and gave Joe a run for his money. You were either a Joe girl or a Nick girl; you couldn't be both. Part of the responsibility of being a Joe girl or a Nick girl was engaging in the never-ending discussion as to who was the true lead singer of the band, Nick or Joe? There could only be one. And unfortunately, it wasn't Kevin.

In my eyes, this conversation was put to bed when Joe was cast as the star of *Camp Rock.* The movie settled the age-old question. Joe was clearly the star; Nick and Kevin were barely in the movie. Seeing Joe Jonas and his long, shiny hair rock out to "Play My Music" was enough to convince me that Joe Jonas was the man of my dreams. It's still one of my favorite Jonas Brothers songs. Every time I hear it, I am reminded of the life I could've had, had fourteen-year-old me met Joe Jonas and convinced him to fall in love with me.

In addition to falling head over heels in love with Joe Jonas, the glory days of the Disney Channel introduced me to a talented young Demi Lovato, Miley Cyrus, and Selena Gomez. My roster of stars to obsess over was expanding. The Disney Channel was in its prime, churning out great musical programming and big stars in the process. I felt so connected to those kids because we were all the same age and the programming was so relatable to my life. I felt like we were all kind of growing up together, even though they didn't know me. But in my mind, we were all on parallel paths. When I was done watching the Disney Channel, they were done working at Disney. It was like we were all going to school together. I was clearly delusional back then and I'm glad to report that absolutely nothing has changed.

But back to Joe Jonas, the object of my young affections. The mere thought of him used to keep me up at night. I just knew I was the perfect girl for him, and the notion that he would, most likely, never meet me left me feeling devastated.

I remember feeling so obsessed with him, to the point that it would make me upset. In the back of my mind, I knew I was never going to marry him. It was physically impossible, and that shattered my heart into millions of pieces.

It's funny and mortifying for me to recall this time in my life because I actually know Joe now, and I *still* think he's the man for me. No disrespect to the gorgeous and talented Sophie Turner by any means. She might *also* be good for him, but I know that he and I had potential. Ultimately, Joe and I both found different paths in life and it worked out. I see him and Sophie at events occasionally, and I respect his marriage and, well, my own self-image, so I would rather die than ever tell him how I used to plan our wedding. Thankfully, he will most likely not be purchasing this book.

My flair for the dramatic translated to my music taste, too. While Olivia stanned *NSYNC and Jackie loved Backstreet Boys, and even Margo became obsessed with Britney Spears, I got into emo music and bands like Secondhand Serenade and The Fray. I would listen to the overwrought ballads in the back of our Ford Explorer and imagine that I was in the music videos for them. You could call it delusional; I call it imaginative.

The strange truth of my teenage fandom is that it was largely internal. I didn't keep scrapbooks of news clippings and photos like most of the girls my age. The biggest demonstration of my devotion was simply a photo of Joe as the background of my desktop computer. While it may seem sane and lovely, I kept my feelings inside because they were so socio-pathic. I would never have put into writing how obsessed I was because it was borderline criminal. If anyone had ever known how much I actually loved the Jonas Brothers, I would have been locked up.

Posters and appreciation from afar are where fandom ended for me as a young girl. When I was a fan of someone as a kid, the most I could do was put up a poster, make their photo my wallpaper on my computer, and beg my parents to take me to a concert. Whereas now, there's much more of a direct line to your celebrity idols. Whether you're an adult or a kid, you can do something that a celebrity sees or they can interact with you at the drop of a hat. It's more fun now because you can love someone so much, and they can know it. But back in the day, you would stand at a concert in the very last row and think that Joe Jonas was looking right at you. That was the only connec-tion you had as you desperately hoped he would jump off the stage and propose because he saw you sitting fifty rows back in an oversized Jonas Brothers T-shirt.

As I got older, the slate of teen dramas I was consuming be-gan to shape how I saw and understood the world. *The OC* and *Mean Girls* became the framework for how I saw everything, but specifically high school. While other girls had pictures of shirtless Zac Efron and Nick Jonas in their lockers, I had pictures of Regina George and Cher Horowitz. I became obsessed with high school and, especially, being popular. If Cady Heron and Marissa Cooper taught me anything, it was that you're nobody unless you're popular. These fictional characters ended up influencing many of my teenage decisions. I guess you could say they were the original influencers.

In fact, when most kids were playing pretend house or kitchen or whatever, my sisters and I would play high school. Instead of choosing roles like mom and dad or teacher and student, we duked it out over who would be cast as the pretty cheerleader and who would land the dreaded role of the geek. Nobody wanted to be cast as a geek. It actually ended up being good preparation for when we got to high school.

The Jonas Brothers were the first, but certainly not the last, phenomenon that provided me with a blurred line between real life and entertainment. When I moved to Manhattan in the eighth grade, it was around the same time that *Gossip Girl* premiered. That show was a movement among my generation, and I quickly became a devoted fan. My friends and I would frequently cut class to watch them film on the streets of New York in the hopes that Chuck Bass might stop and take a photo with us on his way back to his trailer. Being the drama queen that I am, my new life in New York City made me feel like I was a character on the show. At times, I genuinely thought my life was a TV show and that people were watching me. It sounds insane, but as a teenager at a high school in New York City, how could I not think that my life was an episode of *Gossip Girl*?

TV was this constant thing in the back of my mind. I would wake up and imagine there was an audience watching my every move. I would strut down the street feeling very Blair Waldorf, imagining an audience at home watching me look fabulous, when I probably looked like a moose. Everything I was doing, whether I was at school, hanging out with my friends, or talking to boys, felt like it was a show and I was the star. I would brush my teeth and wonder what the audience thought about my brushing my teeth this way. I'd imagine what song would be playing to accompany every little moment of my day. As strange as it sounds—and believe me, I know it's weird—it forced me to do everything with a little extra oomph. Which isn't a bad way to go through life. It probably explains my deep love for reality TV. Or maybe it means I'm just a narcissist who thought my life was so interesting, it warranted a TV show.

You'd think that my affinity for pop culture would have worn off as I got older, but when I got to college, it got worse. I was aging backward. My dorm room looked like what my ten-year-old room should've looked like, with One Direction and Taylor Swift posters covering my walls. The more I understood pop culture, the more I loved it and felt like I should be a part of it. The more TV shows I watched and the more music I listened to, the more obsessed I became. As social media became more a part of my everyday routine, I became more involved in stan-hood and fandoms as I got older, which is weird, because it's typically a childish thing.

The new possibility for fans to be connected with big-time and once-inaccessible celebrities on social media has created this feeling of intimacy. There's a direct conversation being had. We're hearing from our favorite celebrities on a daily, even hourly, basis. Certainly more than we did when I was younger and had to wait for Miley Cyrus to be on *TRL*. And it's not just social media either. Celebrities are doing more interviews, podcasting, and livestreaming. There's so much content that you can engage with. It's a full-time job these days to be a fan. Every day there are hundreds of new interviews, podcasts, press pictures, Instagram stories, and TikToks to watch. You can't help but become obsessed.

The flip side of this close, intimate connection is that the relationship is much less straight worship and more of a two-way communication. Fans now have the ability to know more and, therefore, judge more. We feel like we have a right to be personally offended by a celebrity's actions because we feel like we know them. I thought I knew Miley Cyrus personally back in the day when I was dreaming about being friends with Hannah Montana, but in reality, I knew absolutely nothing about her. I had never even seen her in person. But now I am inundated by Miley Cyrus content. It creates a sense of faux familiarity, which can often breed contempt. That's why it's easy to chop off someone's head when they do something you disagree with. Idols are no longer idols. They're figures on the Internet whom we feel entitled to judge.

Social media has also created a class of fans who are very casual and less devoted than ever before. Fandom takes less effort now. It's easy to follow a celebrity casually and see what they're working on. But you don't care about them that much. It doesn't take any effort to be a follower, and you don't seek out other experiences, such as concerts, live shows, movie premieres, or meetups, because what you get digitally is more than enough. Whereas a real fan is buying concert tickets and merch, listening to hours of podcasts, and showing up in real life. So there's a stark difference between fans and followers, a divide made that much more apparent as more and more people build huge social followings and become "famous."

The new caste of celebrities whose fame is based solely on their number of followers is super interesting to me because I myself am one of them. Instagram and YouTube have created a brand-new marketplace of celebrity. But things get dicey when you have followers because there's an assumption that all those followers are now fans of yours, when that's definitely not the case. I have over three million followers on Instagram, but I certainly don't have three million fans. You can't just assume that all your followers are your fans. There are plenty of people with tons of followers, and nobody knows who the fuck they are because nobody actually cares.

I follow plenty of people on Instagram whom I honestly wouldn't recognize if they slapped me in the face. I chose to follow them because I appreciate their aesthetic or think they're funny. Just because I follow you doesn't mean I'm your fan, and just because you follow me doesn't mean you're my fan either. Over the last eight years, my number one priority has been to convert those followers into fans, whether they connect with the podcast, my comedy, or my Instagram. Because in this day and age it isn't exactly hard to have followers, but it's a whole other thing to have fans.

Take my tour, for example. If, hypothetically, you follow me on Instagram, that doesn't necessarily mean you want to buy tickets to see me do comedy. You might just like to casually see my content in your feed, and that's the extent of our relationship. So when the time came for my foray into stand-up comedy, part of the reason I think the timing was right is because I felt my Instagram following had converted into enough of a fandom through the podcasts and my Instagram stories that I could successfully sell tickets. When your business is built online, either you have a transactional audience or you don't. And you won't know if your audience is transactional until you try. You can have millions of followers, release a line of merchandise, and have only twenty people buy it. Or you could have a smaller following of, say, a hundred thousand people, but they love you and would die for you. You could sell ten thousand shirts. That person with a hundred thousand followers can make more money selling merch, tickets, or even books than a person with ten million followers. It's not always about the numbers, it's about the devotion of the people who follow you. Quantity vs. quality. It's like having ten good friends or one best friend. What's more valuable?

Followings have become a currency for digital personalities and also traditional celebrities. When Britney Spears was the face of Pepsi and her commercials became iconic and hugely popular pieces of Americana, Pepsi didn't know exactly how many people would watch her commercial and, in turn, order a Pepsi because of it. But now, thanks to social media, you can put a price on Britney Spears if she promotes a product on her Instagram because she has twenty-five million followers, and those followers are now digital currency. *Fans* are the ones going to concerts and waiting in line at meet-and-greets. But *followers* have allowed us to digitally monetize people.

It's weird to think about how you can consume everything about a person online but not really know them at all. I put out a lot of raw personal stuff, but I definitely hold back on some of the dark, insecure feelings. Over the years, I've found myself sharing more and more about my life with my community, not only because it's the job I signed up for but also because you can't hide from the Internet. People are smart; the average Instagram follower is also an FBI-level detective. They can sniff out a celebrity pregnancy or a breakup weeks, if not months, in advance. If you are hiding part of who you are, they will call you out in a second. So, why bother?

Certain celebrities have maintained a level of mystery and distance on social media—shout-out to my girl Taylor Swift. Fans see a curated, artistic version of who she is and not much more. We see her as she wants us to see her. It's a carefully crafted piece of who she really is. She maintains a level of personal privacy and doesn't oversaturate fans. Perhaps that's why she has stuck around for so long. Familiarity breeds contempt, and after a while of constant exposure, people start to hate you for no good reason. Remember Anne Hathaway?

I don't take it lightly when people support me, and when they hate me, honestly, I get that, too. Don't forget, I am a fan first. I know what it feels like to love someone and to hate someone. I find myself in a weird position where I am a huge fan of so many people, but I also have fans of my own. So much of my relationship with my fans is based on our mutual love and appreciation for pop culture, so I get the roller-coaster ride we're on together and I try to be real with them.

I am now at a point in my life and my career where I've been able to meet some of the people I obsess over and even become friends with them. As someone who still gets so emo-

tionally invested in celebrities and TV shows that I love, toe-
ing the line between being a friend and being a fan is my cross
to bear in this lifetime. That line became especially challenging to toe after my Instagram started to blow up. I was being invited to events and parties that my favorite celebrities
were being invited to as well. When I scored an invite to the
VanderCrawl bar crawl in 2016, I couldn't stop being a fan.
The event was being put on by Bravo to promote the newest
season of *Vanderpump Rules*. All of the cast members were
there. I was a huge fan of the show, plus almost the entire
cast followed me on Instagram. We had even DM'ed on many
occasions. I spent the entire night in the VIP section freaking
out and trying to carry on normal conversations with people I
absolutely adored. It was the best night of my life. Better than
my bat mitzvah.

Being a huge, if not the biggest, fan of celebrity culture has
certainly helped me along in my career. I am a professional fan;
it's what I do for a living. It's what got me fans of my own. But
the term "fan" is too much of a blanket statement. There are
so many different types of fans. Some are good and healthy,
and some are . . . not. The most premium type of fan you can
be is an OG fan. When you're with someone from the beginning, from their come-up, you feel like a talent scout, iden-
tifying their genius and becoming adamant in your fandom,
even sometimes indignant when others join in. Take my love

for Taylor Swift. I was onto that sweet blond songstress back when she wore spaghetti-strap sundresses and sang earnestly in the back of pickup trucks. Sure, she's a global icon now, but I take pride in the fact that I got to watch her go from playing shows in bars to playing shows at Wembley Stadium. OG fans take pride in the time and effort they invest in their idols. But OG fans often breed a sense of resentment, especially when the bandwagon fans show up. You are a bandwagon fan if when someone reaches critical mass, you jump on the trend. You don't invest much time in someone until they are universally beloved. Let's take Kacey Musgraves, for example. Sure, everyone loves her *now*. How can you not? She played Coachella and won the Grammy for Album of the Year all in the same year. People love her now, but excuse me, I drove two hours to Huntington, Long Island, to see her like six years ago. I am an OG fan and the rest of y'all are a bunch of frauds.

But I've had my fair share of moments when it comes to being a bandwagon bitch. Take Billie Eilish. She's talented and certainly in the zeitgeist right now. Not exactly my jam, but I can't avoid her in pop culture, so I've become a casual bandwagon fan. And I probably only like her because everyone else does.

When I become a fan of someone, I like to get in early. I discover people and I love to watch them grow. I remember watching the Kardashians from season one of the show and connecting with them immediately. I loved that they were sisters. They were so funny and cute. And I really connected with their familial vibe. After season three, BOOM! Enter the bandwagon fans. The Kardashians became so popular, almost overnight, and everyone started to love them just as much as I did. I felt so territorial and almost resentful of their new fandom because I really felt like I was their first and only fan. But obviously life had other plans for them.

I still love the Kardashians, especially Kim, who has evolved so much. I'm really inspired by the way she's handled the adversity and the heartache and the bullshit that have come her way. The people I look up to most in life are constantly evolving, and that is Kim to a T. Her career skyrocketed from a homemade sex tape, but she's working toward becoming a lawyer now and has such different priorities for her work and family life. That's called growth, bitch. I love that because I feel like I'm also so different from the person I used to be. And I'm always evolving and always trying to grow up. Kim is a role model in a lot of ways.

The day Kim's feud with Taylor Swift came to a head was a really hard day for me. I was really conflicted because I truly love them both so much. To this day, I can't even really process the situation entirely because it just hits too close to home. It's hard for me to talk about because if I do choose a side, I feel like I am betraying one of them and all the years I spent supporting them.

Another important fan archetype that can really complicate things is the blindly loyal fan. When you're this type of fan, you love someone regardless of what they do and you just follow them blindly and find yourself apologizing to everyone for their mistakes. I feel this way about many people, but Bethenny Frankel, from *The Real Housewives of New York City*, comes to mind immediately. So much of my job is to watch reality TV, recap it on my podcast, and post about it on my Instagram. With Bethenny, I find myself constantly taking her side and supporting her even when her actions are questionable. I just love and believe in her so much, I refuse to think that anything she does comes from a bad place. Sure, you might think the way she spoke to Carole Radziwill in season 10 on their trip to Cartagena was harsh, but I choose to believe that it's what Bethenny thought was necessary and therefore, I think it was necessary.

Bethenny is also hugely active on social media, which adds an additional layer to my love for her. I kept up with her when the show was off the air and continued to follow her after she left the show. I really feel like I know her. She's incredibly philanthropic and an amazing mother. She's always using her platform for good, especially in the face of tragedy. She's donated and delivered supplies and resources during hurricanes, earthquakes, and wildfires, all while battling for custody of her daughter. She sent more than $17 million in PPE supplies to health care workers and responders during the COVID-19 crisis. With all that I know about her, how can I not blindly support her? I believe in her.

The final level of fandom is the intellectual fan. This type of fan has an intellectual respect and appreciation for someone's contribution to pop culture or society. Take Andy Cohen, for example. I love him, but I really love his *work*. I think he's a genius whose contribution to reality television will live on for years to come. He's created most of my favorite reality shows, and I'd consider him to be one of my biggest inspirations and role models. Having said that, I have never bought tickets to see him on tour and I'd probably never wait in a line to meet him.

Part of being an invested fan is the inevitable conflict you encounter when someone you love does or says something you don't agree with. There are a lot of things you can do when your favorite celebrity or influencer lets you down, but a popular route to take is the troll evolution. The line between love and hate is thin, and many people find themselves crossing that line in the face of celebrity controversy and becoming a troll. Fandom creates a sense of entitlement where fans feel like their favorite celebrity owes them something, and the moment fans disagree with their favorite celebrity, the love they once had becomes an equal amount of hate. They have the energy and dedication of a fan, but they hate you now. It's a cycle where at any moment, your biggest fan can become your biggest detractor. You'd be surprised to learn that most of the people who troll me on a daily basis used to listen to our podcast every day and have seen me on tour multiple times.

That entitlement can manifest itself in entire Reddit threads or Facebook groups devoted to criticizing a person or even a TV show. The *Game of Thrones* ending was widely criticized, as was the final season for its continuity issues. And I get it. I love a good critique just as much as anyone. Remember on *Friends* when Rachel Greene's pregnancy magically lasted well over a year? Or how about when they spelled her name wrong on Ross and Emily's wedding invitation? Or how about when all six of them lived in huge West Village apartments yet were mysteriously never at work? Well, I do, and it still drives me nuts to this day. But to shit on an entire season or the entire franchise of a beloved show and demand the creators release an alternative ending is ridiculous and representative of how toxic and unreasonable that entitlement can get.

I am not proud of it, but I have found myself at times turning into a hater of someone or something I once loved. *Sex and the City* is a prime example of that. I watched it when it originally came out and loved it. Like most young fans, I identified as a Carrie. Her quest to find love and the perfect pair of overpriced heels appealed to me as a young girl. But as an adult, when I watch reruns on E!, I can't make it two minutes without cringing. I now see Carrie for who she really is—a fiscally irresponsible adult who was constantly making bad decisions when it came to both her career and her love life. Back in the day, nobody wanted to be the Miranda of the group—probably because she had a terrible haircut and ended up with a guy who was a foot shorter than her. But Miranda is actually the best character on the show. She is the only sane one with a firm grip on reality. She was the first to buy her own apartment and even decorated with Ralph Lauren paint, for Christ's sake. By the end of the series, she managed to have it all—a flourishing career and family life. She was a true modern woman. Her marriage with Steve was real as fuck and the one viewers could relate to most. Carrie was a self-centered narcissist—who would want to be her? She was a terrible friend. None of the women could ever count on her in the way she could count on them to constantly be there for her.

Over time, it's natural to take a more mature and even critical view of the movies, shows, and celebrities that you love. The way you see the characters and interact with them changes as you get older and as the culture changes. I can't watch some of my favorite episodes of *Friends* without cringing. It's one of my favorite shows, but I can't ignore that most of Monica's story line is rooted in fatphobic rhetoric. There's an entire episode about Ross's fear of and dislike for his male nanny, simply because he's a man. There is also only one Black recurring character in the entire series. So many of the story lines would never get written, let alone produced, today.

. . . So, I couldn't help but wonder (lol) . . . what does it mean to be a fan today? The modern, discerning fan is aware of their icon's flaws and shortcomings and yet celebrates their successes. We don't have to demand unattainable perfection in order to appreciate a great new song or the most attention-grabbing TV show. If we accept a realistic view of humanity, then we can share a real appreciation of artistic accomplishments because of imperfections, not in spite of them.

CHAPTER SEVEN

When the Fan Becomes Famous

If there's one thing I know for sure, it's that I was meant to be famous. I've always loved an audience and I've always craved the kind of attention and validation that comes from hearing thunderous applause, or seeing the likes rack up on Instagram, or being stopped by fans in the street. Whether it's in the halls of Ramaz Upper School or the pages of Instagram, I want everyone to like me and think I'm cool, funny, and smart. But as they say, man plans and God laughs.

I feel weird referring to myself as a famous person because I genuinely like to think of myself as a regular chubby girl with a little ketchup on my shirt and a questionable number of days between hair washings. But if being famous is defined as being known about by many people, then I guess I am considered famous. I think once you get a book deal you can officially call yourself famous.

The first time I ever felt famous was in 2015. I was at a casino in Puerto Rico. Ben and I used to fly down to San Juan once a year to get sunburned and blow all of our cash at the blackjack table. When a girlfriend of one of the players asked if I was Girl With No Job, I was floored. Nobody had ever recognized me from my Instagram before. I was slightly horrified when she asked for a photo because I was sitting at a table with five middle-aged men who had no idea what was going on. They spent the entire rest of the night asking me millions of questions, confused how I could be famous if I had "no job."

Since then, I've grown comfortable with the idea that people recognize me in public—it's one of my favorite parts of my job. I know how shallow that sounds, but to know that someone is excited to meet me, in the way that I've been excited to meet celebrities, makes me feel really special. I know that, particularly in New York, people will know who I am the moment I leave my apartment, and I'm okay with that, even when I look like a beast. It's very on-brand for me to be spotted walking my dog in a robe, with no undies on. For the most part, fans approach me to say they enjoy the podcast, they've followed me for a while, and they're glad to finally see me on their trip to New York, like

I'm the Jewish Statue of Liberty. It's always overwhelmingly positive and really sweet and meaningful to me.

Of course, sometimes people are absolute animals and it gets dicey. I once had a young woman fully come and sit at my table during a meal, refuse to leave, and then order her own dinner. In her defense, I did invite her to sit down for a minute to chat, but I didn't think she was going to stay until dessert. She never left! All night long. And I didn't say anything because I never want to be known as a bitch. Those are the stories that people remember. So I just kept quiet and let her stay.

For the first few years of my newfound fame, I got to experience all the perks of what it means to be a celebrity. Brands pay you to show up places and do virtually nothing, people come up to you at restaurants and concerts and ask for photos, and if you play your cards right, you can even parlay a small bit of fame into friendships with fellow celebrities. For a pop culture nut like me, that is by far the best perk of all.

The first celebrity I really became friends with is Paris Hilton. We met on a crazy trip to Mexico a few years ago and developed an actual friendship after that. I flew down to Punta Mita for a friend's birthday celebration weekend. Every year for her birthday, she invites a huge group of people down to Mexico for the weekend, including some stragglers and hangers-on like me. It's a group full of real A-listers. Previous guests have included Gwyneth Paltrow and Leonardo DiCaprio. All different sorts of agents, business types, and fashion insiders score invites, and some years, even chubby Instagram stars with a penchant for tequila.

Paris and I connected almost immediately because, first of all, she followed me on Instagram. That's always easy access for me. When a mutual friend introduced us, I knew instantly that I wanted to be her friend. I knew she was a fun-loving gal like me and that we'd hit it off. We all *think* we know everything about our favorite celebrities, so I was ready to meet the Paris I thought I knew—an heiress and professional party girl. In reality, she's one of the coolest, funniest, and smartest people I've ever met. We spent the next few days together, and I got an inside look into the genius that is Paris Hilton. She has such a large presence for such a small person. She lit up every room she walked into. When she invited me back to her hotel room one evening, I made sure to take note of everything. I wanted to know what the life of a true celebrity looked like.

I was shook by the sheer amount of suitcases she was able to load onto a private plane. She'd brought seven suitcases. She had over thirty pairs of sunglasses organized in an acrylic case. One of her suitcases was devoted to her DJ equipment, because she was DJing one of the after-parties that weekend. She seemed like such a famous person, given the amount of designer clothing she'd brought, and yet, on the flip side, she acted like a totally normal girl you'd go to college with. As I watched her get ready for dinner (not in a weird way, she invited me), she sprayed me with her Paris Hilton perfume, and that's when I knew we were real friends. We exchanged numbers before I went back to New York, and we've been friends ever since.

When you're able to take a celebrity friendship from Instagram messages to iMessage, that's when you know you've made it. My collection of celebrity phone numbers is something near and dear to me. I consider it to be one of my greatest accomplishments. From Gwyneth Paltrow to David Foster, I have managed to collect quite a roster of phone numbers, although I never dare to actually use them.

The one thing about fame that has both pleasantly surprised me and disappointed me is the people. I've talked to some of the most genuinely lovely, nice people whom I never would have met if it weren't for the Internet. I'm constantly surprised by my followers and how great they are. But at the same time, I'm constantly disappointed by people on the Internet because they can be truly awful and cruel. It's a sword that swings both ways. You can't have one without the other. I hate to complain and even acknowledge those people, but unfortunately, they get to me. A lot. I know how unreasonable it sounds to want everyone in the world to love me, but considering my long history with striving for popularity, it's difficult to deal with the negativity sometimes.

Being a public figure really fulfills a need for me, but being so disliked and somehow becoming this polarizing, controversial figure kills me. That's the part that I can't deal with. That's the part that keeps me up at night constantly. I'm actually disliked by a lot of people, and I struggle with that so deeply. Of course, part of that is my own doing. I have said some really dumb things that have made people, even some of my biggest fans, turn on me. I am so hard on myself as a result. With each "controversy," I get further and further from the career I envisioned for myself. I do my best to continue to be unfiltered, funny, and outrageous, but in this climate, that can be challenging sometimes, and more often than not, I find myself in hot water with my fans.

I understand that negativity and backlash is just par for the course when it comes to my job, the job I chose. I take a lot of it and try to let it roll off my back. But every few months, something happens and I crack. It unleashes a wave of anxiety and depression where I don't want to leave my bed for fear of misstepping again. I have fantasies about quitting my job because I just feel like I can't handle it. I can't imagine having to be put under a microscope for the rest of my life. I know that this is what I signed up for. I'm sure everyone feels this way to some extent, but there are moments when I want to give it all up. The highs of fame are very high, but the lows are so low, and they take a real toll on my mental health and my ability to be the funny, effervescent, bubbly person I have always been.

If being famous is defined as being recognizable—both you personally and your work—then I acknowledge that opinions and judgments are part of being known. Observation is an inherent part of fame. I would hope, as anyone with any sort of following hopes, that the awareness is positive, but that's not always the case. It's unrealistic to think that everyone who knows you is going to love you. You can't will universal love into existence. Trust me, I've tried.

There's a phenomenon of people thinking because you're famous, you've signed a social contract that says absolutely nothing in your life can be off-limits anymore. And as a fan of many people, I subscribe to that notion. I want to know everything about Taylor Swift, from what she ate for breakfast to when her next album is coming out. But as someone who's recently entered the world of celebrity and whose private life is nonexistent, I also disagree with the notion that celebrities aren't entitled to privacy. Privacy is necessary and should be respected for people whether they're famous or not. Remember when the paparazzi photographed Bethenny Frankel at her fiancé's funeral? They followed her to the cemetery, hid in the bushes, and photographed her crying at the private burial? It was in that moment that I realized nobody is entitled to privacy anymore and it's incredibly fucked up.

When you are Internet famous, you owe a lot of your success to the people who follow you, and they know that. They can use their support as a weapon, because they know they can take it away at any given moment. Whereas if you're a musician and someone likes your music, there's not really the same level of entitlement to have access and then to judge your personal life. Their music made them famous and that's what they owe their fans; the rest is just gravy. People like Taylor Swift are given the freedom to keep certain parts of their life private. But Internet stars got successful by letting people in. I became who I am by opening up my life, livestreaming from the bathtub—how can I not share everything else?

There's this pressure from people who are constantly wanting me to share more, open up more, and post, post, post. When I do just that, and post more personal and revealing information, it gets picked apart. I put so much of myself out there, which people can connect with, but they also can take advantage of my vulnerability. It's this endless cycle to give more, but when I do, I wish I never had.

I'm definitely not one of those people who complains about being famous, because at the end of the day, I love my life and I am so grateful for all the things that have been afforded to me because of my platform. People who complain about fame are generally annoying and sound out of touch because they know what they signed up for, especially when it comes to social media notoriety. So even though it may sound like I complain a lot, I am eternally thankful for the life I have been given. I am also just a natural complainer; it's the Jew in me. Forgive me.

I have to admit, my skin isn't nearly as thick as I used to think it was. I can't handle a lot of the backlash I receive. I feel like every time I do something controversial or make a mistake, the fallout is on a higher level than it should be, especially when I'm not even remotely as well-known as other people who have gotten called out for the same thing. Becoming famous on the Internet makes people feel intimately close to you because you're giving them so much more access. Social media stars release more personal and raw content than traditional celebrities, and they do so more frequently. I think that people hold Internet personalities to higher standards than they do traditional celebrities because Internet stars are essentially real people. They're more relatable to fans, which makes us all feel more connected.

I see it in the way people comment on James Charles, for instance. He is by no means unproblematic, but let's all remember that he's just a kid. By twenty years old, he went from a local makeup artist to the first male face of CoverGirl and a YouTube sensation with almost twenty million followers. He was invited to the Met Gala last year, which is the ultimate sign you've arrived. When he got called out by Tati Westbrook, a fellow makeup artist and YouTuber, for certain shady business dealings and disloyalty around vitamin promotions (how 2019, amirite?), he got it bad. His "controversy" was worldwide news. He trended on Twitter for days. Thanks to social media, this incident is going to follow him for the rest of his life. He'll be associated with Tati's accusations forever, all because of something that happened to him when he was twenty years old. I am by no means a James Charles apologist, but it's interesting to see the level of discussion and subsequent fallout that happened around him when people like Chris Brown seem to skate by without nearly as much public scrutiny.

Tati Westbrook has since released a video recanting the allegations and apologizing to James Charles. What can't be recanted is all the mean tweets about him in 2019. You can't recant all of the brand sponsorships and YouTube subscribers that he lost. You certainly can't recant all of his "friends" who unfollowed him on social media, can you?

The way that people react to "real" celebrities seems relatively light when you compare it to the reactions to a social media star's situation. Somehow, every influencer and Internet star is now controversial in one way or another. They lose deals and opportunities all the time because of it. Yet Alec Baldwin and his career seem to move on completely unscathed. He's starring in new movies and TV shows constantly. How many times are we going to give him a break?

The Internet did not invent celebrity culture—but it did change it. Even traditional celebrities become more famous as their social media communities grow. They're able to get projects green-lit, to land bigger roles and deals when they can show the bigwigs that they're bringing their own huge fan bases to the table with concrete social media numbers. Actors with big social followings are far more likely to get a role than someone else, simply because they have twelve million followers and the other person doesn't. It increases their value in Hollywood. And new talent can be discovered outside of the traditional (and nearly impossible) routes. Shawn Mendes, for example, got famous on Vine (RIP). He didn't wait for a record label A & R executive to find him. He could have been some loser in Toronto for the rest of his life. Now he's just a loser in LA wearing expensive women's vests.

There are a lot of double-edged-sword components of fame, specifically Internet fame. On the one hand, you can be discovered through social media and find traditional success through having an online community. On the other hand, you are held to a different, nearly impossible, standard. You need to be successful while also being relatable. You need to share your life, but not so much that you become overexposed and ultimately resented. You need to always say and do the right thing, because if you accidentally show the world that you are a human who makes mistakes, you will be immediately cancelled. Brands won't want to work with you because you'll now be considered radioactive, and the opportunities that were once knocking on your door will now be on to the next person (until they fuck up, too).

That toxicity extends beyond your professional life and even into parts of your social life. People are afraid to be associated with that kind of controversy, and those you once considered friends are expected to speak out and condemn your actions publicly. If they don't, it can result in residual cancellations for them. It's pretty wild. Never underestimate the power of a Twitter mob.

Social media has changed what it means to be famous. It's not just about looking great on a magazine cover or on a red carpet, but also allowing a certain amount of access into your home and personal life. Back in the day, celebrities were able to walk the red carpet a few times a year and do a couple of interviews. It was harder to become famous and there were fewer celebrities, but they were afforded quite a bit of privacy compared to today. Now it's much easier to gain a following and become famous, but it requires more access to your personal life. Take the kid singing sensation Mason Ramsey, for example. Now he is a bona fide country singer, and last year he was singing in Walmart! That wouldn't have been possible twenty years ago.

There will always be a separation between traditional and digital talent. Traditional celebrities—the actors, musicians, and comedians of the world—hold that coveted A-list spot. Everyone wants it, but hardly anyone can get it. Some digital talents (very few) have successfully transitioned into traditional celebrities. Lilly Singh went from YouTube to NBC. Chiara Ferragni went from influencer to international fashion icon. But traditional success is no longer the goal for everyone. Internet stars are making just as much money as traditional celebrities, and they're almost as, if not more, famous.

It's always been my dream to become a mainstream celebrity and transition from digital to traditional media. Couldn't you see me as a daytime talk show host? Or a late-night commentator? Or perhaps a budding sexpot actress? Maybe you can't see it, but I can. I always have. However, the more that I work and the more that I grow, the more comfortable I feel in the digital space. I don't feel like I'm missing out on anything. I have the opportunity to be creative, to be in control of what I do and put out into the world, and I have the most amazing community to connect with. I don't have a record label or a movie studio to answer to. Within minutes, I can connect with people all around the world and make a living doing that. Why would I want to change that? Plus, I already struggle so much with the modicum of fame that I do have that I don't even know if I could handle becoming a TV star. But listen, Andy Cohen, call me if you need another late-night host on Bravo, mmkay?

There's an underlying concern among digital stars that this bubble is someday going to burst. If history has taught us anything, it's that all good things must come to an end—remember MySpace? "Influencing" is an oversaturated market and it feels like at some point this bubble is going to burst. Truthfully, I don't feel that way. There are so many different types of people who are looking for different types of role models, inspiration, and entertainment. The Internet is the perfect place for them to find everything and everyone they're looking for, so there's an unlimited number of people who can and will become famous because of the Internet. I don't think there will ever be enough.

The tricky thing with fame can be the money that comes along with it. We've seen what a money-hungry celeb is willing to do in a pinch (hi, Depends commercial, how are ya?). And the sad truth is: I get it. There are very few things I wouldn't do for money. Fortunately, I have a good radar when it comes to deciding which jobs to accept and which not to accept. I think about the big picture and where a job will lead me down the road rather than just thinking about the paycheck. Sometimes turning down opportunities is beneficial in the long run. I turned down an episode of *Maury* in 2016 because I didn't think it was the right opportunity for me, and I haven't looked back since. Because I've worked and achieved a lifestyle that I'm comfortable with, I no longer have to take gigs because I need them. Now I take them because I think they would be good for my career, fulfilling or challenging in some way, or just plain fun. But who knows? I could be one controversy away from needing to do porn. I could make a killing doing BBW.

Sometimes you have to say yes to an opportunity as a stepping stone even if it's not financially a huge win. Sometimes I work not for money but to raise my star. A lot of deals that get you on TV raise your profile but offer you no money. So you've got to balance those deals with the shitty deals that no one hears about but make you a good amount of money. I did a Grammys red-carpet recap for E! a little while ago. Normally I wouldn't say yes to an offer that didn't pay me, but it was a part of an overall partnership, and obviously I thought it would be great for my brand to be on the E! network talking about celebrities. It was exactly what I wanted to be doing even though I wasn't being compensated. To have said no, simply because of money, would have been silly.

One of the largest misconceptions about fame is that everyone who's famous is rich. So many celebrities who appear to be pretty famous are actually financially unwell. One doesn't necessarily lead to the other. If I had to choose, I would rather be rich than famous, because there's so much instability when it comes to fame. Money gives you the freedom to not give a fuck about what anyone thinks about you. With extreme celebrity, you have all the attention, scrutiny, and lack of privacy but not necessarily the financial freedom to escape it. Just ask Kate Gosselin.

The second time I felt famous was in 2016 at the roast of Rob Lowe on Comedy Central. Ben and I were invited by Comedy Central to work the red carpet and host Facebook Live coverage of the carpet. They were looking for a bigger digital presence for the event. It was a star-studded affair and we were right in the middle of it. I had never been on a red carpet before, and of course, my biggest concern was how I was going to look. My insecurity was at an all-time high, so I spent the days leading up to it drinking tons and tons of water. If I couldn't get skinny in three days, I could at least have clear skin. This was one of those times I wasn't feeling great about myself and I agonized over what to wear. I tried to plan my outfit before leaving for LA because I have so much trouble getting dressed, it would have been so irresponsible of me to fly across the country without knowing exactly what I was going to wear.

I ended up hating my outfit and running to Zara on the day of the show to find something better. I landed on this sort of ugly, unflattering black dress with a metallic silver bomber jacket from the Zara men's department. I looked like a piece of tinfoil. Comedy Central had arranged hair and makeup for me, which really made me feel like a star. It gave me confidence even though my outfit made me look like a glorified baked potato.

It was my first experience at a legitimate Hollywood event. It was fabulous! I had watched many red carpets on TV, but to be there in person was a whole other experience. There were so many A-list stars walking around, like Pete Davidson, David Spade, Rob Riggle, and Peyton Manning, among others. Ben and I had a huge camera crew set up on the red carpet and we were positioned as the first stop for celebrities walking the carpet. We were interviewing people as soon as they arrived. I remember one of our first interviews was with Jeff Ross, who was hosting the roast. He showed up in a Prince costume, to honor the late singer, who had recently died. When he explained his costume to me, I interpreted it as *a prince*, not the man Prince. I literally had no idea who he was dressed as or what the fuck he was talking about. I felt so out of my depth.

I didn't actually get to meet Rob Lowe, which I was okay with because I didn't fully know who he was. At the roast there were all these jokes about his making a sex tape with a sixteen-year-old and I remembering thinking, *Why are we celebrating this person?* I guess I was a little ahead of my time.

When I got back to New York, I made the terrible decision to read every single comment on the Facebook Live. Facebook can be a nasty place. But Comedy Central's Facebook page is particularly vile. It consisted mostly of disgusting old men exclusively commenting on my body. I wanted to die. It was a special corner of the Internet, one that I hope never to see again.

Overall it was a great partnership with great exposure and a great paycheck. It was my first time walking a red carpet and the first time Ben and I got to do something together. I loved traveling with him, of course, and I enjoyed working alongside him for the most part. He was super nervous, and while at home I am the nurturing and comforting wife of his dreams, on set I was of no help. I couldn't help him. It was his first experience being on camera and he was very anxious about the interviews. I laid it out to him plain and simple and told him: "I don't have the time to comfort you. I've got to worry about myself; get it together!" I love him, he's my life partner and the future father of my children, but I've got a career to worry about. You're on your own on this one, Ben.

I have to give Ben credit, though. He has acclimated to the celebrity Instagrammer life pretty well since we got together. When we first started dating, Girl With No Job was gaining a lot of traction, and when we got serious romantically, it was blowing up. I was obsessed with checking Instagram. I would spend all day scrolling through my followers and noting the new celebrities who'd followed me. I spent the first two years of our relationship exclusively scrolling Instagram. At the time, there weren't any third-party programs to help sort through your followers for you. Back then, you'd have to manually just scroll through all your new followers. I was spending so much time making content, posting content, and living on Instagram. It was nonstop and, as was made clear to me, really annoying for Ben. I had to get him off my back somehow, so I started brainstorming. I had a 90 percent female following and I wanted to expand my brand without disrupting the feminine space I'd curated. I had the idea to start a page called Boy With No Job, which would be content geared toward men. I figured Ben could get started with it while I thought about how to handle it long term. I had intended to hire someone to run the account but Ben ran with it. We started to like working alongside each other and Ben was really good at it.

I love that I have brought Ben into the fold, and my sisters, too. With the expansion of *The Morning Toast* and Toast News Network, we've been able to give Margo and Olivia their own podcasts. It's been great for business and for our family. We have this mutual love for our brand, and it's definitely brought us all closer. But I feel a responsibility to constantly monitor what everyone's posting, especially Ben, because if he fucks up, I'll feel like his spokesperson. I've dragged everyone into this clusterfuck and unfortunately, I sometimes bear the burden when shit goes awry.

Ben brings a lot of his own talents to the table besides that chiseled jawline. He is very cool. People meet him and they're just instantly drawn in. He's super charming, and when he's chatting at events, he's so funny and personable—the definition of a great networker. I'll meet someone famous and never see them again. I am too embarrassed to pursue anything outside of that initial conversation. But Ben exchanges information, connects in this casual but confident way, and always makes a follow-up plan. He creates relationships out of quick introductions, and he's always pushing me to be better at that. In those situations, my introverted side comes out, and I feel a little self-conscious, because I know I don't belong. Ben's encouragement is great, if a little annoying.

It's hard for me to focus on the few negatives of fame when I've gotten some of the most incredible opportunities because of it. Probably the most unbelievable experience I've had with a celebrity was on that same trip to Mexico where I met Paris. I was invited to spend the day on a yacht with a few people, one of them being Leonardo DiCaprio. I know, insane. I had read about what goes down on these celebrity yacht trips, so I was ready for a day full of alcohol-induced debauchery. But, unfortunately, it was nothing of the sort. Leo is actually incredibly low-key. I was hoping to see Leo in his Jordan Belfort element, drinking up a storm and snorting coke off of my ass, but he did neither. He wanted to play backgammon and go whale watching, so that's what we did. He wanted to jump off the top of the yacht and swim to shore, so that's what we did. Yes, Leonardo DiCaprio saw *me* in a bathing suit. I'm sure he wasn't even looking but it still counts. I nearly drowned halfway to shore because we completely underestimated the distance. Upon arrival at the beach, I was too out of breath to do anything, so I just laid there like a beached whale.

Although my outing with Leo was not nearly what I expected, I was still overjoyed to have been invited. I can now say that I have been on a yacht with Leonardo DiCaprio. Nobody can take that away from me. After our average day on the open seas, we got back on the very small dinghy to go ashore. The moment we got on the dinghy, the sky turned dark and ominous. A big-ass storm was coming. We were on this tiny boat, rocking back and forth between some of the biggest waves I'd ever seen in my life. For a moment, I genuinely thought we weren't going to make it and all I could think of was the inevitable headlines about our death: "Leonardo DiCaprio and Unidentified Chubby Brunette Die in Fatal Boating Accident." Instead of starting to cry, which is what I wanted to do, I took the opportunity to make a joke. I started singing, "Near, far, wherever you are . . . ," in my best Celine Dion voice and Leo actually laughed at my joke. It was kind of iconic.

Being invited to star-studded parties is by far my favorite perk of celebrity. I'm not talking about the industry parties with red carpets and press. I'm talking about the low-key parties. The house parties. Like a party hosted by Robert Pattinson that I somehow stumbled into. I was in LA for business and tagged along with a friend to a "party in the hills." Sounds good to me! After a windy, vomit-inducing drive through the Hollywood Hills, we walked into a party at a very unassuming house. And all of a sudden, there was Robert Pattinson standing by the door. He thanked us for coming to his party and showed us to the bar. I was shook. He was so skinny and pale. As the resident *Twilight* stan, I couldn't believe I was talking to Edward fucking Cullen. I so badly wanted to ask him to bite my neck, but I refrained. I stood silently as he talked to my friends, relieved he wasn't acknowledging me because I was not prepared to respond.

Throughout the night, as I continued to meet new people, everyone would ask: how do you know Rob? Obviously I responded: I know him from my *Twilight*-fueled sexy-vampire fantasies. How about you?

I was thrilled to be there but felt so out of place. I found myself with nobody to talk to, because who the fuck would talk to me? I ended up falling into a conversation with a much older couple in their sixties because that's where I felt safe. They looked like nobodies, so we had that in common. The woman told me she was an author, and her husband was a filmmaker, and they worked together. When I asked what movies they had worked on, they said a little franchise called *Fifty Shades of Grey*. It was E. L. James and her husband. I had no idea. Who knows what E. L. James looks like? And why the fuck was she at Robert Pattinson's party?!

As out of place as I felt, I was also finally feeling comfortable in my own skin for the first time in five years. I had just gotten my chin procedure and lost a lot of weight, so I was really feeling myself. I was wearing a striped blouse from Boohoo, Topshop jeans, and Gucci sneakers. Giving off a very casual cool vibe. It feels good to get ready to go out for the night and feel comfortable and confident.

Miley Cyrus and Liam Hemsworth were there, as were Pete Davidson and Ariana Grande. Ariana and Pete had been dating for a month; they were national news and this was the height of their relationship. I had spent the previous week gabbing about them nonstop on the podcast. I couldn't believe I was in their presence. Their relationship was everywhere, confounding and intriguing millions of pop culture connoisseurs. That night, Ariana was perched on Pete's lap, drinking a glass of red wine, and showing off her new, enormous engagement ring. I was SHOOKETH! This news wasn't out there yet, and yet here I was, sipping my tequila mere feet away from the biggest pop culture news of the year. It was a private party at someone's home, so I made the very difficult decision to respect the celebrity code and not post about the news. I did, of course, text my sisters. What can I say? I am human.

I knew how unbelievable it was to be there, and I felt so in awe of what was going on around me. I wanted to remember it all, which was difficult because these parties have unlimited access to top-shelf alcohol. I made the decision to black out, but I was strategic about it. After every drink, I'd text my sisters a play-by-play of what was going on around me so I didn't forget in the morning. I wanted to enjoy the party but the fangirl in me couldn't let it go.

When I'm in LA, I'm a permanent tagalong with my cool friends. I just go where they tell me to go. I don't get invited to things myself. The same weekend as the Robert Pattinson party, I also tagged along to Seth MacFarlane's birthday party at a hotel in West Hollywood. I had one mission, and one mission only, that night: to ask Seth when *Ted 3* was coming out. Kidding, I'd rather die.

It was Halloween weekend but Seth's party wasn't a costume party. Normally, I wouldn't have cared, but I was going to a Halloween party afterward. Instead of wearing my costume to Seth's, I decided to leave my costume with the hotel concierge and change before the next party. I was so relieved I'd ended up wearing my street clothes, because there were three people at Seth's party in costume, and they looked so weird. I actually felt bad for them.

I changed in the hotel bathroom into a really cute Pink Lady costume that I had ordered on Amazon and had shipped to my hotel in LA. I may have been running in fancy circles, but I wasn't above buying clothing on Amazon. I'm still not. Thank God it looked decent. Our next stop was an actual Halloween party at some big fancy house. I expected the house to be covered in Halloween decorations, but the only ghosts I saw were the wide-eyed cokeheads stumbling around the property. What the party lacked in decor, it made up for in celebrities. It was star-studded. The Foster sisters and Gwyneth Paltrow, among many. Oh, Joe Jonas and Sophie Turner were there, too. That was a tough pill for me to swallow. They looked so cute and happy—it killed me. *Could've been me.*

The next morning, I went back to the hotel where Seth had held his party. When I went to pick up my bag from the concierge, it was missing. It had mysteriously vanished without any explanation. Goodbye Gucci shoes and Boohoo blouse. I was devastated and utterly confused. I've seen *The Bling Ring*; I know thievery is common in Hollywood. But at a five-star hotel? Seemed weird.

Another one of my favorite trips to LA was when Ben got an opportunity to partner with the NBA for All-Star Weekend. I tagged along because I had my own stuff to do in LA, and who am I to turn down a free first-class trip to LA? After one of the festivities from All-Star Weekend, we were at a party at some Hollywood agent's house. It was a truly sickening house. Rich. As I beelined for the bar, obviously, I ran into my boss from my Verizon show *The Morning Breath*. This was before Verizon royally cancelled our show, so I was pleasantly surprised to see my boss. He was sitting on a couch talking to Elon Musk, whom he is somehow friends with, and I stopped in my tracks out of sheer surprise. He introduced me to Elon, saying, "This is Claudia. She runs Girl With No Job." And Elon perked up and said, "Oh my God, I love your blog!" I couldn't breathe. I mean, I didn't even blog anymore but who was I to correct Elon Musk? I wasn't about to ruin my only chance at going to space.

When I'm at these parties, it's a tug-of-war inside me. As a fan and pop culture commentator, I'm swooning over the celebrity sightings and inside look at Hollywood. I wish I could document it all and share with my followers. It's so painful because this is the content that I'm dying for and that I know my audience is dying for. But I refuse to be the girl at the party taking pictures. These are parties, not work events, and it's really just a bunch of friends getting together. They're not taking pictures. They're just trying to enjoy their lives, so I don't want to disrespect that. I'm never going to be the girl sneaking pictures because that's just embarrassing and a huge breach of trust. If you're invited, it's under the pretense that you're going to respect that boundary.

As my inner fangirl was fighting to publicly freak out over the unbelievable scenes I witnessed, I wanted to respect their boundaries. Which I did. Until right now.

What's so strange about these parties is how normal it all is. It looks like a high school party, just with nicer houses and bartenders. There's this illusion—and I bought into it for a while—that the Hollywood social scene is this debauched, hedonistic inner circle where at any given time there is wild sex, drugs, and, fuck it, rock and roll. When you show up to a party like this, either at someone's private home or at a hotel or restaurant, there are paparazzi outside and often security or staff working the door and checking people in off a list. But once you're inside, it's really just a party with famous people milling about. Honestly, not to sound incredibly spoiled and jaded, but sometimes it's a little boring. Everyone at the party is talking about the most famous person in the room, and if you're talking to the most famous person, they're talking about themselves. Everyone spends the night looking over their shoulder wondering where the biggest celebrity is. It gets boring after an hour.

What's not boring is the food. In my experience, these casual house parties are always catered affairs where nobody actually eats the decadent spread: racks of lamb, a dozen different salads and sides. And again, no one eats it. The sheer volume of food is astounding. It's like they didn't know how many people were going to be there, but they wanted to make sure that if fifty thousand people showed up, they could feed them.

Everyone mostly mingles, relaxes, and grabs another drink from an eager-to-please, good-looking bartender. Most of the time people are smoking pot, and some are casually leaning over a coffee table to enjoy a line of coke. Edibles are also a big offering at parties, whether it be weed or 'shrooms, so I have to be really careful I don't end up high off my ass when I'm going in for a decadent snack, as I often do. I prefer to do drugs in the comfort of my own home with people I trust, not in front of A-list celebrities. I don't think Hollywood is ready for me to be a shrieking lunatic on LSD.

I love being invited to those parties and events because I used to read about them in *People* magazine and see them on social media. Just like anything in life, fame has its perks and its disadvantages. At the end of the day, this is the life that I chose for myself, and although there are parts of it that I don't like, I'm not ever going to stop trying to be successful. I was made for this life. How mad can I really be? It's easier to swallow the additional scrutiny and lack of privacy when you're blacking out at Robert Pattinson's house.

Fame is a fickle food, after all. And, as usual, I've got a mighty big appetite!

CHAPTER EIGHT

You're Either Going to Love Me or Hate Me

The last few years have seen the rise of one of the most alarming (and annoying) cultural phenomena: cancel culture. Whether a celebrity missteps, misspeaks, or commits an actual crime, they're tried in the court of public opinion and—often too quickly—deemed *cancelled*, or over. Cancellation is often followed by the ceremonial stripping of someone's cultural cachet and subsequently, their relevance. If done properly, it can be devastating and can result in the ending of their career. Suddenly, all of their success seems to be dismissed because it was somehow built on a throne of lies.

How do I know so much about cancel culture? I'm glad you asked. It's because I had the grave misfortune of being cancelled not too long ago.

On the morning of February 28, 2018, after a drunken night out at Luann de Lesseps's opening night of *Countess and Friends*, I woke up to more than just a hangover. The Daily Beast released an article where, for the first time, they publicly connected me to my mom and her political views. Spoiler alert: She's a conservative. A proud one. It wasn't necessarily a secret who my mother was, it just wasn't something I always shouted from the rooftops, given the immense danger it could have put me and my sisters in. When ISIS issues a death threat against your mother, you don't exactly write "That's my mom" in your Instagram bio.

The same day the article was published, old tweets of mine, from years before, were posted all over Twitter. They were racist and abhorrent tweets, disguised as jokes. I hate to even use the word "joke" because they weren't funny. They were the thoughts of a dumb sixteen-year-old trying to sound edgy. In addition to the recent headlines about who my mother was, the media painted a picture of who they believed me to be. They thought they had revealed who I truly was. Within minutes, my horrible tweets were everywhere on social media and reported widely on news and pop culture sites. It was my worst fear realized. Before I had time to fully recover from my hangover, I was cancelled.

As if things couldn't get any worse, the day that all of this happened was also the day my sister Jackie got engaged. And just because my life was falling apart, it didn't mean that the weeks of planning were going to be put on hold. The world, unfortunately, didn't revolve around me. We were all supposed to be getting ready for the big engagement party that day but I was too busy having a breakdown, refreshing Twitter every two seconds, to put makeup on.

I arrived at the engagement party wearing no makeup and sobbing. My family and all of my sister's soon-to-be in-laws were in the back of Cipriani in a party room, celebrating my sister's engagement. My head was spinning. I knew I had to connect with my fans . . . just as soon as the party ended. I did my absolute best to not make a scene and wanted my sister to enjoy what should've been one of the most special days of her life. I already felt like shit; ruining my sister's big day would've been the cherry on top of the shit sundae.

After the big moment and champagne toasts, I ran home, put on my pajamas, and recorded a video. I wrote nothing in advance; I knew what I wanted to say and I had to just get it out there. I needed to be direct, be honest, and—most important— apologize. It took me a couple of tries to get through it without breaking down. I looked puffy and ugly and couldn't have cared less. I knew that for every second I didn't address what was going on, I was disappointing more and more people.

I looked at the whole shit storm from the perspective of what I would want from someone I follow and admire. If somebody I loved made horrible jokes about Jews, what would I need them to say in order for me to forgive them? In the midst of a controversy, I had seen tons of celebrities issue apologies from their publicists, but it never seemed sincere to me. I really wanted people to know that I didn't feel this way. I wanted them to know that my tweets from high school were not a reflection of the twenty-three-year-old woman they knew. I was mortified and ashamed. I knew my fans wanted to hear from me, and not in a polished statement from a publicist that could've been written by anyone. I hired a crisis PR firm that my lawyer recommended. They required a $25,000 retainer. I realize now what a mistake that was, but I was desperate for anyone to help fix the mess I had made. After wiring them the money, I proceeded to ignore everything they told me to do. I didn't agree with any of their tactics. They wanted me to go dark for months and then do an interview on *Good Morning America*. I knew this wasn't the right move.

The video I recorded was about as raw and vulnerable as anything I've ever posted online. I spoke directly into the camera, with no makeup and still puffy from crying.

Some really disgusting, vile, stupid tweets of mine have resurfaced. I need to just come right out and say how sorry I am.

It's not cool; it's not funny. I was a dumb kid; I was sixteen. I thought I was being funny and cool on Twitter.

But I took responsibility. I apologized. I condemned my words as the thoughtless, hurtful sentiments of a teen trying to make waves online. I asked my followers if they would give me the chance to make it up to them in time. And I apologized again.

I am so sorry to anyone who read those tweets and had a reaction and was upset, because you're totally entitled to that reaction. But it's so important for you guys to know that's not who I am. And if you give me the opportunity to show you who I am and what I stand for, I would be so grateful. But I understand that these things take time and what I did was not okay. I'm so sorry.

It was my most naked moment on the Internet. I look back now on how I handled it, and even though it was uncomfortable and embarrassing, I'm proud of it and I wouldn't change a thing about the apology.

I think there was an expectation that I would publicly disparage and disassociate myself from my mother in the video, which I didn't. I never even thought about it. To this day, people still try to shame me into speaking out against my mom. If you picked up this book hoping to read a scathing chapter on my mom, you're going to be disappointed. It will never happen. It's not who I am; I wasn't raised like that, and I hope you weren't raised that way either. The way people demanded, and continue to demand, that I speak out against my only living parent says way more about them than it does about me. Family is too important to me, and neither politics nor fame changes that.

Additionally, I think it sets a dangerous precedent when we expect people to take responsibility for statements they didn't make themselves. No one is demanding that Ireland Baldwin publicly condemn the actions and statements of her father, are they?

I can only take responsibility for the things that I do and say. I am not responsible for anyone else's views and nobody is responsible for mine. I didn't feel it was necessary to publicly speak ill of the woman who gave me life simply because it was what others wanted to hear. The Ten Commandments are so ingrained in me. I repeated them constantly as a kid, whether in temple or at school. "Honor thy mother and thy father."

Growing up with a mother who worked as a political journalist gave me a firsthand look at just how ugly politics and the media can get. And I immediately wanted nothing to do with it. I found it shocking at a young age that adults could get so bent out of shape over politics.

As if the petty in-fighting within our political system wasn't enough to grapple with as a teenager, we also faced legitimate danger as we received death threats from major foreign terrorist organizations. Between the state-of-the-art security system in our house and two failed assassination attempts over the years, you can imagine how terrified I was when the media put my private family life on blast. I had never been more afraid for my life than I was when that Daily Beast article came out.

The media claimed I had "hidden" who my mother was for superficial reasons, like protecting my reputation and my career. But the real reason I never publicly addressed my mother's identity is because of the immense amount of danger it placed me and my sisters in. That article put the ultimate target on my back.

When I put the video up, all that mattered to me was taking responsibility for my actions and apologizing. If my career had ended and that was the last thing I ever posted, I would have felt my integrity was intact. I was proud of the sincerity and openness of the video, and that's what mattered most. It wasn't easy to be that vulnerable and raw, but I knew it was the right thing to do.

I kept the comments enabled on my post because I wanted to hear from my fans, and I wanted them to feel like if they needed to call me out, they had the chance. This was about them, too. I wasn't going to take the easy way out, even though my management team at the time told me to turn them off. I think people respected that I wasn't hiding. I was taking full accountability for my actions, no matter the cost.

Well, I posted it in the evening and then went to bed pretty soon after. The first people who saw it were the people who followed me and supported me, and the comments were really reassuring. It seemed like they were feeling the genuineness of the video. I thought that maybe, by morning, the news cycle would've flushed my irrelevant ass back down the drain.

I woke up to the exact opposite, actually. It had been picked up on several news outlets and my inbox was full of press inquiries. *The View* wanted me to come on. I love Whoopi Goldberg, but *The View* is the scariest place on TV. I turned it down immediately. My comments section on Instagram was flooded with people who didn't know who I was before, didn't follow me, and knew nothing about me. They just hated me and had no intention of changing their minds. They automatically hated me because some "reporter" on Twitter had told them to. But that's kind of how the Internet works. The loudest voices don't necessarily reflect how the masses feel.

That feeling of remorse is one I'll never forget. I felt so mortified by the person I used to be. It was a weird feeling because I was taking responsibility for the actions of a person I no longer was. I felt so disassociated from my teenage self yet was taking the heat for her actions. I was full of shame. I also felt helpless, because even though everyone was telling me not to, I was reading every tweet, article, and post written about me. I couldn't help it. There was so much misinformation being spread about me and my family. It was infuriating to just sit by and let strangers speak about us that way.

For the rest of my life, I will be sorry that I said those things. I'm not here to cause anyone pain; that's the antithesis of everything I do. As someone who has craved universal love and adoration for her entire life, I was heartbroken when I suddenly became universally hated. All I have ever wanted is to be well-liked; that's part of the reason I got into this line of work. I always knew that my personality type was not everyone's cup of tea, and in the beginning of my career I struggled with people's finding me too loud or too annoying. But after my cancellation, there was a new, bigger, and louder group of people who hated me because they believed I was racist and ignorant. It created a huge group of people who hated me, and that was one of the things I struggled with the most. I felt so misunderstood. I still do.

Overnight, I had become this polarizing figure. The mention of my name caused drama. I couldn't believe it. I still can't believe that that's my life. I am definitely in denial about that to this day. My presence on podcasts or at events is still controversial. I spend most of my time in a state of anxiety, thinking of ways I can change it. But the truth is that I can't. That stigma of being socially and professionally radioactive rarely goes away.

After I posted the video on February 28, 2018, I had to live through the immediate fallout of my cancellation. The day after my apology, my agents at CAA called me first thing in the morning. When agents in LA are calling you at nine a.m. in New York, you know it's not good news. They told me that Verizon had cancelled our show, *The Morning Breath*, effective immediately. I did everything I could to not cry before hanging up the phone. I got that dreaded lump in my throat and started bawling the second I hung up. Verizon was also planning on releasing a statement about the cancellation. I knew that would reignite the news circuit and that this nightmare was far from over.

After my agent called, I got a call every hour from my manager, each to let me know about brands that no longer wanted to work with me. By the end of the day, every single brand I was working with at the time had decided to drop me. Chase, Diet Coke, and Diageo were the first of many brands to dissociate from me. Most of the brands I was working with at the time claimed that I had breached our contract's morality clause. When Facetune decided not to move forward on a deal we were negotiating, I was crushed. That one was a particularly hard pill to swallow.

Shortly thereafter, my agents at CAA dropped me altogether. I kind of understood since an agent's sole focus is to bring in money and I was no longer making any. I was not a lucrative client for CAA. So even though I was sad to be dropped, I understood why. Even so, my point agent there was one of my very close friends and still is. He was the one to call me and let me know that the bosses upstairs had decided to drop me as a client. We both just cried on the phone. It felt like the last day of camp.

A few days later my manager dropped me as well. That was a tough blow. It felt like I was being abandoned on this sinking ship. Unlike an agent, a manager's focus isn't just to make you money. They're there to help navigate the decisions and growth of your business along the way. So to me, this was the moment I felt like I was radioactive, like I'd never work again. People on Twitter were rejoicing at the news of all the members of my team abandoning me. None of it felt real; I couldn't be present enough to understand what was really happening because it felt like such a nightmare. The six years of hard work that had gone into building my business felt like a complete waste of time. I just sat on my couch, screaming.

Ben was really there for me even though I could barely look him in the eye. He was working at a big media agency at the time and was getting phone calls from his office questioning him about what was going on. I was unintentionally taking everyone down with me, and that was one of the hardest parts. Margo was named in every news article—how in the hell was she supposed to get a job after college? Olivia wasn't fired from AOL but had to go into the office and deal with the scrutiny and eyeballs from everyone at the company. She called us from the bathroom crying on her first day back. I felt terrible.

I had been in bed for a week, wallowing in my own self-pity, when I got a text message from professional Kardashian BFF and self-proclaimed "Food God" Jonathan Cheban that made me laugh out loud. Not "lol" but actually laugh out loud. He said, "You better stop competing with me for 'Page Six' placements. I had three yesterday, do not try to outdo me. LOL JK. Are you ok?" I'm not entirely sure if he was trying to make me feel better, but something about the way he spoke about the press so casually made me feel like maybe the world wasn't going to end. Maybe this was just what it was like to be famous.

I had lost about ninety thousand followers. To think that that many people were offended, hurt, and turning away from me made me really sad. I decided to take some time off. I was so mentally drained from the cancellation that I needed to step away. I was also no longer working and was too embarrassed to see any of my friends. I didn't leave my apartment because I was afraid my doorman had read "Page Six." I was the talk of the town, both in print and in digital, and New York had never felt smaller. I knew I had to get out of town and take a little time away from what was feeling like a minefield of shame. I spent some time in Utah with my family. Overnight, we had become the most scandalous family in America. I couldn't have gotten through that time without them. They were the only people I could be around without feeling ashamed. It felt like they were the only people who knew the real me and what was truly in my heart. I've always been incredibly grateful for my family but in that moment, I felt especially thankful.

It sounds so cliché, but it was really peaceful to be one with nature in Utah. With spotty phone service, it was easier to unplug and drown out the noise. I really enjoyed it. I felt like it opened my eyes to how big the world is and how small my problems were. It also gave me a reinforced appreciation for my family. Now we go back to Utah once a year; it's one of our favorite places. After that trip, I spent a lot of time at home, hiding out and just being so embarrassed. I still couldn't look my doorman in the eye.

My friends didn't know how to handle the situation either. They just were so shook, because they live private lives and couldn't relate to what I was going through. They were texting and checking in on me, but I think they felt weird. I felt weird. I felt embarrassed. I had been the cool friend who got everyone tickets to *Watch What Happens Live* and invited them to fun parties. Now I was a national joke. I really didn't want to see anyone, even though I was grateful they were all checking in.

Unexpectedly, one of the most pivotal moments of that time was a short phone call I had with Nicole Richie. Surprisingly, she had heard nothing about my cancellation but offered to give me her two cents. We had stayed in touch since filming *Candidly Nicole* in 2015, so when a mutual friend offered to set up a phone call, I jumped at the chance. Nicole has been on the cover of every tabloid in America since 2010, so I figured she might have some insight. I could handle the highs of celebrity, but the lows proved to be more than I could stomach. I wasn't entirely sure this was what I wanted for my life. Suddenly, a regular job didn't seem so bad after all.

Nicole made me laugh, a lot. She gave me really good advice, and I trusted her because who knows more about bad press than her? She encouraged me to get back out there and be myself, with a better understanding of how impactful my platform is. She assured me that bad press is par for the course when you're in the public eye, and as long as I didn't let it get to me too much, I would be okay.

After a few weeks, Jackie and I were ready to put ourselves back out there. We loved working together, we couldn't deny our dynamic on-screen, and we couldn't let go of our dream of being morning show hosts. So we started a new show called *The Morning Toast*, which launched on April 9, 2018. Our show on Verizon had had this amazing set with a professional production and crew. And we wanted to emulate that in our new show, but we had just lost all of our income and we no longer had the backing of a major media company. We couldn't put together that type of show. We pooled our resources, took what we knew about production and podcasting, and tried to make it work independently. We thought of a name, secured the Instagram handle, and announced it on Instagram. We were back.

Sitting in my chair next to Jackie that first day of filming *The Morning Toast* was a really big milestone for me. I had made it through one of the most difficult experiences of my life, learned more the hard way than I had ever thought possible, and come out the other side. I would never be the same, but I was okay with that. I was stronger and smarter for it. I wanted *The Morning Toast* to be everything *The Morning Breath* wasn't. As a person, and a host, I had a new sense of empathy and understanding that I felt empowered by. I was an entirely different person. I had a whole new perspective on things, specifically cancel culture, and after weeks of hiding, I was ready to share it with the world.

- - - - - - - - - - -

The most fucked-up part of the cancellation process is the rejoicing that occurs when the angry mobs of Twitter trolls successfully cancel someone. There's a ceremonial dancing on their graves. A lot of people on Twitter live for a public shaming. They can't wait to tear people down, often forgetting that people—yes, even celebrities—are human beings. As someone who has reported on many of pop culture's biggest cancellations and also has been cancelled herself, I can offer a unique perspective on why we like to engage in the public teardowns of our favorite celebrities and influencers.

Social justice warriors and the PC police on Twitter have made it their responsibility to right all the wrongs in the world, when literally nobody asked them to. What started as a genuine attempt to eradicate prejudice and bigotry took a weird turn somewhere and gave us cancel culture. Ironically, it ended up making the world a more negative, hateful place. It seems so odd to me that so many people find joy in scrolling down someone's social media page for hours just to find something incriminating from ten years ago. What are you doing? No offense, but that doesn't make you a social justice warrior, it just makes you a loser. Every single person on the planet has said something dumb in their past. If you're calling someone out on Twitter, trying to "expose" them, odds are you are guilty of a similar offense. So you're perpetuating a toxic culture that will one day take you down with it. We all have skeletons in our closet no matter how many followers we have on social media.

Publicly doxing someone, publishing their address and putting a target on their back because they said something ignorant, is not going to teach them why their language was hurtful. Don't get me wrong; people need to be held accountable for things that they have said, but there's a way to have an open, productive dialogue that would result in more positive change.

It's okay to have said something ignorant in your past as long as you now understand why it was ignorant. For me, my ignorance was rooted in my youth and my desire to be edgy and funny. I grew up with a lack of understanding of the world around me. That's evident when you read my old tweets. It's okay to not know everything as long as you're willing to learn and grow from your experiences, particularly regarding how language and assumptions, among other things, can hurt people. There is so much value in civil discourse, and in this climate, we need it more than ever. People are too quick to jump all over each other, attack, name-call, and ultimately, cancel one another. Pretty soon, there will be no celebrities or influencers left, because nobody's perfect.

The culture is so vastly different from what it used to be. We are all more woke and progressive, which is amazing. As a society, we have a better understanding of experiences different from ours. We are more vocal about fighting for equality. But it's important to remember how far we've come. Half the stuff they played on TV in the early 2000s would never, ever get aired today; that's how much things have changed. The first few seasons of *Entourage* featured tons of gay slurs and nobody thought twice about it in 2004. If a TV show used a gay slur today, there'd be a ton of outrage. And deservedly so! When our culture has obviously shifted, how can we hold somebody's 2010 remarks to a 2020 standard? It seems unfair.

I haven't always been this understanding and reasonable, though. Like Ramona Singer, I am renewed. I used to be that person who loved putting people on blast, calling them out the second they did or said something wrong. And in that moment, I genuinely thought I was doing the right thing. That's why I don't totally discredit people who constantly criticize and bully me online. I know that they genuinely think they are doing the right thing in hating me, and sometimes they even make some valid points about my behavior. Even though I shouldn't, I read every comment, thread, and post written about me. Sure, it takes a major toll on my mental health, but every now and then a troll makes a valid point, and I want to be self-aware enough to keep growing and learning. Before 2018, I didn't realize how much of an impact the things I did or said could have. I now realize the impact, and that realization came the hard way.

In my opinion, a heartfelt apology and signs of genuine remorse should be enough to give someone a second chance. During a celebrity scandal, sometimes the public cares more about how you handle it than the actual offense. You can change hearts and minds if you are willing to humble yourself and put in the work. I remember watching Jonah Hill on Jimmy Fallon in 2014. He had been caught on camera making a terrible homophobic remark to a paparazzo who was harassing him. He got called out online pretty badly. He immediately went on *The Tonight Show* to address the situation. I remember watching and thinking he was so earnest and truly sorry for what he had said. He didn't bother with excuses or with a formal statement from his publicist. He took the more humbling road of apologizing directly, which is difficult, instead of posting some typed-out message on social media. And when you think of Jonah Hill you probably don't even remember this incident. Nobody even knows that he almost got cancelled.

It never really affected him or his career because he owned his mistake, and from the tremble in his voice, you could tell he was so sorry. That's why Kevin Hart's nonapology was so shocking to me. We're so used to the same routine—cancel, apologize, reform, repeat. But Kevin refused to apologize at first, because he claimed he had apologized so many times in the past for the same joke. Part of me agreed with him and respected his decision to step away from the Oscars. How many times must a person's history get rehashed before we officially bury it? The other part of me saw so many members of the Black and LGBTQ+ community who needed to hear him apologize again, and I sympathized with them, too.

Unfortunately, my cancellation still affects me and my business to this day. I miss out on brand deals all the time because of it. I lost a huge opportunity with a major streaming service for my comedy special because I was too controversial. I can't shake my past, and while it's frustrating, in some ways, I feel like the cancellation was one of the best things that ever happened to me. As much as I'd like to erase it from history, some wonderful things happened because of it.

Emotionally, it made me a much more sensitive and mature person. It taught me not to discredit people's feelings and how to listen to others. It taught me how big my platform is and, more important, that I needed to be more responsible with it. It taught me that I am not always right, I'm usually wrong.

It taught me to value other people's opinions and feelings. It taught me that I wasn't doing enough with my platform.

It's really a tough thing to go through, especially at a young age, when you're so obsessed with what people say about you. When you're twenty-three and all you want is to be universally well-liked and you end up being universally disliked, that can be devastating. Nobody's universally beloved, and to learn that in a very hard, public way forces you to grow up. It was tough in the moment, but now I look back on that whole experience with a positive outlook. It totally changed me. I love who I am now, and I couldn't have become this person without it.

Professionally, the cancellation led me to take control of my business and restructure in a way where I wasn't relying on other people or companies to stay afloat. Before the cancellation, my entire revenue stream was based on the hope that a brand would want to work with me. Now *The Morning Toast* and Toast News Network are their own self-sufficient companies with multiple revenue streams, including ad revenue, merch, and live events. I never wanted to put myself in that vulnerable position again, where at any moment, everything could be taken away from me. I wanted something real, something stable.

I want to move past everything that happened to me, and I don't want it to be what I am known for. But I will always take responsibility for my actions. If someone came up to me, now or when I'm ninety years old, and told me they were personally hurt by my tweets, I would apologize wholeheartedly. People's feelings matter to me now, especially the feelings of people who care about me and take part in my community.

Cancel culture is so toxic because it misses all nuances. We cancel people so frequently that it's almost lost its value. We cancel people instead of educating them. And we no longer separate the people who do bad things from the people who say bad things. The court of public opinion groups together all people who have been cancelled. They're putting the Kevin Harts of the world in the same basket as the Kevin Spaceys of the world, even though the two men are completely different. There's a difference between *saying* something offensive and *doing* something offensive, and it's important that we not forget that.

Furthermore, there's a difference between someone saying something bad today and having said something bad ten years ago. I am against cancel culture but I am pro-accountability. No matter when you said something, if you are sorry about it, you should apologize. Period. But the opinions and tweets of your early life should not define you. I refuse to let mine define me.

Society tends to discredit someone's success because of something they did ten years ago, and to me, that's so invalid. At the same time, there are people, especially within the corrupt Hollywood system, who have contributed to a lot of injustice, inequality, abuse, and worse with no repercussions. Cancellation is a spectrum, and it's so hard to navigate everything that's come forward in the last couple of years. There are plenty of known predators who haven't been cancelled within Hollywood. They're still actively working and raking in money. It's so strange. "Cancellations" are not one-size-fits-all, and they should be judged on a case-by-case basis.

Ellen DeGeneres is a perfect example. Up until a year ago, she was the face of kindness. She received the Medal of Honor from President Obama. She's a real LGBTQ+ icon, as she portrayed the first openly gay woman on television. She is an important cultural figure, and it seems like she's using her platform to highlight important stories and to give back to communities all around the world. But it's recently come to light that it's not all as good as it seems. Allegations came out that she treats her employees terribly and is considered "one of the meanest people alive" by some of those who work for her.

Should that undo all the money she's given away? The veterans she's helped? Or the LGBTQ+ people whose work she's inspired? Honestly, I don't know. She's the perfect example of someone who has done good for the world and been a pioneer but who is—allegedly—a nightmare. It's ironic. Her brand on the show is kindness. She ends each episode of her show by reminding her audience to be kind to one another, for fuck's sake!

Since this news broke, I've really stopped watching her stuff on Ellentube or engaging with her online. How I reconcile that is that I don't necessarily want to strip her of all her accomplishments, but I don't find myself really wanting to support her in an intimate way anymore.

Being an asshole is not a crime, so there's not more to say about Ellen. Chris Brown is another story. He is a known abuser but still has a record label releasing his music. Kendall Jenner was in one of his recent music videos. What the fuck? It seems like the world has amnesia when it comes to certain celebrities and what they can get away with. In my eyes, there are certain things that are unforgivable. Not everything can be buried in blind fandom. Ellen gets ridiculed online ten times more than Chris Brown does—how does that make any sense? Once again, there's a difference between saying something bad and doing something bad.

Actress, activist, and queen Jameela Jamil is such a great voice for how to be "woke" but also forgiving of our humanity. I am obsessed with her because she's one of the few people who speaks about cancel culture from a human perspective. Jameela understands that nobody's perfect, not even Hannah Montana.

All you can find is progress and not perfection and so that's what we should all be striving towards. Ten years ago I was problematic in my thinking and there were loads of things I didn't know and didn't understand and thought I was right about. Had I been "cancelled" at that time I would never have gone on to become someone who spends all of their life fighting for women's rights and the rights of people who are marginalized and who is now being able to get Instagram and Facebook to change their global policy to protect young people.

—Jameela Jamil

I love this so much because it's so true and I relate to it on such a deep level. I am mortified by some of the things I thought and said as a teenager, and if the world had written me off entirely back then, I wouldn't be the person I am now. And I love the person I am now! I am far from perfect, and I still don't always say the right thing, but I grow and learn every day.

What was so frustrating about my cancellation—and cancel culture in general—was that all these people tweeting at me, writing articles, calling me all sorts of names, weren't personally affected by my words. They weren't offended. They were just excited to take me down. That sucks, and that's not the world I want to live in. That's not the community I want to continue to build. All my followers watched me go through that very public situation and handle it with some grace, in a way that people could respect. Hopefully they learned their own lessons about operating in the world with a little more grace and understanding.

As we launched *The Morning Toast* and I reengaged with my followers, I was so much more grateful for literally every person who I used to just take for granted. I'm so grateful for them because I lost that connection for a while, and I didn't think it was going to ever come back. And now our bond is even stronger. I don't take that for granted.

Having been in that position, and having seen so much misinformation spread about me, I'm reminded that the people we talk about are just people, even if they're famous. They have kids, they have parents, they're just people. It wasn't until I was actually in the hot seat that I realized the way I reported on stuff was destructive. I used to literally refer to Shakira as an anti-Semite because, years ago, I heard somewhere that she was. And right after my cancellation, I actually did the smallest bit of research and found out that was untrue. For years, I had literally been telling everyone that Shakira was a known anti-Semite. Damn! That's how misinformation spreads in two fucking seconds. I have a responsibility to be better than that. We all do.

These days, I've become something of an expert on this subject. I get interviewed a lot on cancel culture, given what I went through. I feel weird speaking on it sometimes because I myself was cancelled. I have these mortifying tweets; I don't feel like I can or should ever call out anyone else because it's like the pot calling the kettle black. When interviewed, I like to stress how important apologizing is. Everyone is entitled to make mistakes, but in order to be forgiven, you need to truly understand why what you said was so hurtful. Releasing a written statement and going dark for a few weeks doesn't show true remorse.

Take time to understand why your words were hurtful, listen to people who are correcting you, and educate yourself on why your thinking was problematic. Pushing up your sleeves and taking the harder route is the right thing to do, and in the long run, you'll be better off for it.

I don't call people out anymore in the way that I used to because I know what it's like to be on the receiving end of it. Even if someone's backlash is warranted, which Lord knows mine was, I don't ever want to make anyone feel the way I felt when it seemed like the world had turned on me. I now find myself reporting on these types of stories and trying to advocate for the person being cancelled. It's in my nature now to give people the benefit of the doubt because I so desperately wanted someone to do the same for me. My new style of reporting usually results in people's being upset with me for sympathizing with the person being cancelled. Then people want to cancel me for my opinions on the cancellation. It's a vicious cycle of cancellation.

But more than that, I've come to learn and truly believe that most of the time, someone's "offensive tweet" is usually a result of their merely not being educated. And if that's the case, shouldn't we be helping them? Teaching them? In the last few years, I've become way more sensitive to this idea. If we shut people down the moment they make a mistake, that leaves no room for progress. Odds are they could really benefit from taking a moment to stop and learn about why what they said was wrong and hurtful.

Because what does it really mean to be woke? Or politically correct? What is the goal here? I used to think everything was lame—showing emotion was lame, sensitivity was lame. But now I'm much more aware of how my words impact others, and I am sensitive to the way that we all interact with each other online and in real life. I'm just more empathetic these days. I'm so receptive to hearing from people if something I've said has offended them or hurt them in some way. I used to brush that shit off. I hate to pander to people who just feel like every time I say something that rubs them the wrong way they need to message me about it, but I have such an intimate relationship with my followers that I never want someone to tune into the podcast and get sad. It's supposed to serve the opposite purpose.

For example, in my stand-up, podcasts, and morning show, I talk all the time about the fact that I have the worst memory. No joke, I have the brain capacity of a ninety-six-year-old. I used to joke and attribute my poor memory to dementia. I received a few messages from people who were angry at me for making a joke out of dementia, a serious disease. I didn't think much of it because honestly, it's a fucking joke! But I got a particular gut-wrenching message from a fan whose father was struggling with dementia. She explained how painful it's been for her and her family to slowly watch her father's brain deteriorate. She went in depth on what it's like to see someone you love completely forget who you are. It was heartbreaking. She explained why my joke really upset her. In that moment, I totally got it. I saw the potential hurt my joke could cause, and I was so willing to change it and learn from my mistake. The idea of this girl's watching our show and constantly being reminded of the pain that her father is in was enough to make me stop. Moving forward, I decided that when I make a joke about my memory, which I do all the time, on the podcast or on tour, I'm going to say that I have amnesia instead of dementia, because that is less likely to offend people. I was ignorant of the potential insensitivity in a joke, and through a civilized dialogue with someone affected by it, I learned and I changed. It's not that complicated. Side note: I have since learned that my lack of memory is not a symptom of early onset dementia or amnesia. After a few meetings with a therapist, I have learned that my childhood trauma has caused me to subconsciously suppress parts of my memory. But that's a story for another book.

When it comes to comedy, there is so much nuance to what offends people and what they find therapeutic. I feel very strongly that it's okay to make jokes about things that make you sad. It's often a way of coping or trying to make sense of something serious. Not everything is going to appeal to everyone, though. If I make a joke about grief in a comedy show, because I personally have experience with it and I'm trying to work through it, some of the audience who is also dealing with grief might find comfort and camaraderie in the ability to laugh at it. But the other half might feel it's too insensitive and sad for them to hear. I am now very sensitive to that dichotomy and I try to walk that line as much as possible.

But often, when someone is offended by or disagrees with what I say, they come at me much more aggressively. "How dare you, you fat bitch!" isn't the start of a respectful and educational discourse. It's not going to help anyone understand and grow. When we can all be respectful and communicative, and a little less trigger-happy about calling each other names, I think we can all learn a lot from each other.

We do a segment on *The Morning Toast* called "Dear Toasters." It's an advice segment where we, most of the time, give terrible advice to our listeners who find themselves in precarious situations. Once Jackie and I responded to an entry from one of our listeners who was worried that a guy she was seeing had an STD.

After the show I received a message from a male listener taking umbrage with something I'd said during the segment. A Toaster had written in about a guy she was seeing who had recently gotten chlamydia. While giving advice, I suggested that she ask him to send a photo of his tests results proving that he's now clean.

I almost scrolled past the message but something pulled me into opening it. It ended up being the most well-written and thoughtful message educating me about my word choice around the issue of STDs. It read in part:

> I know that no way would either of you intend to insult but the usage of clean in terms of STDs has a negative connotation, implying that the individual who does have an STD is dirty. In lieu of dirty or clean, negative and positive is the preferred verbiage. It's generally more of a thing when it comes to HIV in the gay community, but wanted to bring that to light for future situations where an STI may come up as a topic of discussion.

I wrote back almost immediately and thanked him for taking the time to explain the implications of my word choice in such a respectful way and not immediately assuming that my misstep was indicative of my being homophobic. When I said "clean" on the air, I knew it sounded weird, but I couldn't put my finger on why. I really appreciated the opportunity to learn and change the way I address things going forward. This may sound so trivial, but there's value in being kind. I think we all forget that.

That kind of civil discourse is such a rarity in the culture right now. I don't claim to know everything. I can only speak from my own experiences and my own point of view. I'm not gay, and I'm not Black, and I can't speak to those experiences. I know what would offend me as a woman and as a Jew. That's pretty much it. I'm limited by my life experience. So, as simple as it sounds, someone just reaching out and explaining to me why what I said rubbed them the wrong way is so helpful. I can totally respect that. I can empathize and I can definitely change my ways. The issue arises when we come at each other aggressively, calling names and tearing people down for not knowing better. That's not constructive. And that's not going to move us forward in any real way.

After the immediate fallout of the 2018 disaster, I struggled, and continue to struggle, privately with an overwhelming sense of shame and self-hatred. A lot of people are assholes when they're in high school and college, but they get to grow and evolve past it privately. I wake up most days and am constantly reminded of the person I used to be. I'm not her anymore—at all. And, if I'm being honest, I hate the person I used to be. I hate the lack of empathy I had for others. I hate the lack of understanding I had for the world around me. I hate the way I thought the world literally revolved around me. Letting go of that shame and learning to go easier on myself is something I am still working on. It doesn't come easy for me. I, so badly, want to be perceived as perfect, but the joke's on me, I guess.

We're all learning and growing, and I love my Toast community for standing with me during the most challenging months of my life. It feels like we're all finally moving forward, and we're doing it together. I've had the opportunity to grow up in the public eye, which obviously has its privileges, but it also has its downsides. You've seen me stumble and fall big-time, and I'm really grateful to everyone who believed in me and didn't just believe everything they read online.

Just because you said something ten years ago, it doesn't mean it reflects how you feel today. Think back to an outfit you wore ten years ago. I would be mortified to wear gaucho pants today, but in seventh grade, you couldn't stop me from rocking my doody-brown gaucho pants. Now I'd rather die than be caught dead wearing a pair. That's called growth, and we're all entitled to it.

CHAPTER NINE

From Cancelled to Comedy

I didn't become an award-winning comedian overnight. It was more like over a year. Stand-up was
always something I wanted to do but was way too embarrassed
to do. My whole life, I'd been told how funny I was, and I knew
I was funny, but I just didn't think I had what it took to be a
comedian. My fear of rejection was standing in my way. I was
terrified by the possibility of being onstage and saying a joke
that no one laughed at. I have way too much pride to put myself
in that position. The possibility of that vision's ever becoming
my reality was enough to stop me from pursuing comedy professionally for a long time.

I'm a strange person, because I'm super outgoing, brazen, and sometimes even shameless, but there's a part of me that tends to be more introverted. I can become crippled with self-doubt, constantly putting myself down and letting my insecurities get in the way. But, at the same time, I am also the most confident person in the room. I never thought it was possible to be both an introvert and an extrovert, yet here I am. So stand-up was something I thought I could never do but also secretly knew I'd be very good at.

I am not easily motivated, which is why I've worked out six times total in my life. It's also why I waited so long to try my hand at comedy. There were a few things that motivated me to finally get my act together (literally). I first felt the itch in 2016, when I was watching the fifth season of *Shahs of Sunset* on Bravo. Reza Farahan, the protagonist and my favorite character, made the brave decision to try stand-up for the first time. In front of all his friends, his family, and a Bravo camera crew—he just went for it. He had no comedy experience or training. I remember being taken aback by his willingness to try something new and be so vulnerable in front of people. I remember feeling jealous watching him walk out onstage. He was conquering his fears, and I was sitting on my couch eating Baked Lay's.

Unfortunately, his set was garbage and there were hardly any laughs for the entire six minutes. It was painful to watch because it was a literal portrayal of my worst fears. It ended up further deterring me from physically getting my ass off the couch and doing anything. But I like to think that pivotal moment in pop culture planted a seed in me that would later sprout.

At the beginning of 2018, my career was starting to burn out a little. As an Internet personality, you have to constantly be evolving because the industry is constantly evolving. Every day, there's a new fifteen-year-old dancing on TikTok for millions of people, so it's important to keep your content fresh and new. Whether it's creating different types of content or trying new platforms, you have to keep moving. I had a really strong fan base from both my Instagram and my show *The Morning Breath*, but I needed to keep shifting lanes. I refused to get comfortable. I wanted to reinvent myself, and thought it would be both funny and effective for me to try new career paths while documenting the journey on Instagram. I wanted my followers to feel like they were a part of the journey.

First up, I tried to become a DJ. I spent thousands of dollars on equipment and DJ lessons at Scratch DJ Academy before I realized that the DJ life wasn't for me. I couldn't book a gig to save my life. Plus, I was a terrible DJ. The first, and last, gig I landed was at 310 Bowery. The free alcohol made it difficult for me to do my job. I just wanted to dance and drink, not work. I couldn't wrap my mind around being at a club and not blacking out with my friends. The whole thing didn't make sense to me. The check I got from my first gig covered the cost of my equipment and DJ lessons, so I decided to wash my hands of the DJ scene and move on to greener pastures.

After my failed attempt to become the female Diplo, I tried the next best thing—being a YouTuber. If JoJo Siwa could do it, why couldn't I? A few weeks later, I launched my Girl With No Job YouTube channel. I had successful Instagram and Snapchat accounts; how hard could a YouTube channel be? Very hard, actually. My videos weren't funny. Or interesting. Or cool. They were actually pretty cringeworthy. I was scraping the bottom of the barrel every week for new video ideas. The channel flopped almost instantly, not only because the content was terrible, but also because I failed to deliver videos every week. The editing process took so fucking long.

I was failing at almost everything I tried, but documenting the process on Instagram became shtick for me. Though it was funny at first, I hated the feeling of being a joke to everyone. It was getting a little tired. So I called up my manager at the time and said, "I want to do a live show." I was hesitant to call my show "stand-up" because I felt, in some way, it would be an affront to actual stand-up comedians. They write thousands of jokes and spend years, if not decades, refining their craft onstage. They've performed hundreds of times, they've bombed hundreds of times. So I didn't want to brand myself as a stand-up comedian quite yet, because I had no right to do so. I hadn't earned it yet. I labeled it a "variety show" and left it open to interpretation.

I wasn't exactly sure what I was going to perform, but I didn't concern myself with that. I was entirely sure nobody would buy tickets to the show, so I'd never have to figure out what the show actually entailed. It would, yet again, be a funny thing I failed at. Classic me!

My friends and family all thought it was a great idea. I'd always been funny, and this seemed like a natural next step for a funny person. Having their blessing made it easier for me to move forward with the idea. I am incapable of making decisions on my own. I can't leave my house without FaceTiming all my sisters to make sure they like my outfit.

I was shook to my core to find out that the historic comedy club Carolines on Broadway was willing to host my first show. I was under the impression that old-school comedy folks wanted nothing to do with the likes of me and my Internet brand. But the booker at Carolines was so gracious and lovely, partly because, based on my following on social media, she thought I could sell the tickets. The pit in my stomach grew six sizes that day, because part of me genuinely thought nobody was going to come. Yes, I had millions of followers, but did I have fans? There's a difference. Like I said before, just because you have a follower doesn't mean you have a fan. Getting people from the Internet to show up for you in real life is a borderline-impossible task—I was pretty sure people liked my Instagram but almost certain they didn't like *me*. My imposter syndrome was flaring up big-time.

When I put the tickets up for sale, my jaw hit the floor when we sold out almost immediately. I ended up adding two more shows for a total of three nights at Carolines. I couldn't believe it. Was I actually going to do something funny *and* successful for once? It couldn't be!

Leading up to that moment, my biggest concern was actually getting people in the door. Now that the tickets had sold, I had to fucking *perform*. I never thought the tickets would sell but once they did, I realized that I needed to write a show that kept three hundred drunks entertained for ninety minutes. Mind you, I had never written a joke before in my life. I was funny, but being funny does not a comedian make. Some of the funniest people I know would never make it as comedians, and some of the funniest comedians are boring as fuck at a dinner party. I knew I was conversationally funny, in a class-clown kind of way, but by no means did that mean that I had what it took to be a successful stand-up comedian. I had a month to put something together, because whether I liked it or not, people were coming to see me do comedy.

Part of the watermelon-sized pit in my stomach was attributable to the fact that *real* people were going to see my *real* body in person. And to make matters worse, I had to find an outfit that was both flattering and comfortable. When your entire life exists on the Internet, it's easy to get comfortable and rely on apps like Facetune and Photoshop when you're feeling insecure. I've been very vocal about my affinity for Facetune because I want to prepare people for when they actually meet me. Expectations need to be set.

People were going to be seeing my actual body, live and in living color, and that fucking terrified me. Looking back on it, it's kind of tragic how I couldn't even be excited or happy about a monumental moment in my career because I was too focused on the audience's seeing my unedited double chin. It's so fucked up. What's even more fucked up is that that feeling hasn't gone away. If anything, it's gotten worse. The week leading up to the first show, I felt so uneasy about the whole thing. I couldn't sleep and was barely eating—both of which are rare for me.

I was too busy trying to put together a show to even think about finding something to wear. I decided to perform in a pair of pajamas and slippers. Partially because I thought it was a cute, on-brand thing for me to do but mostly because the pajamas were stretchy, comfortable, and, most important, breathable. I wasn't interested in taking on the anxiety of having to put together a real outfit with real clothes from a real store. I didn't want to walk onstage wearing two girdles and a strapless bra. The black pajamas from Amazon were going to have to work.

I blacked out that first night at Carolines, and it wasn't the type of blackout I was used to. Nope, this blackout included no tequila. It was all fear. I had never been so petrified in my life.

When I walked out onstage at Carolines for the first time, something strange happened. My nerves completely disappeared. I leaned into the sweet sound of applause and knew I wanted to hear more of it. As I got to center stage and felt the heat from the spotlight hit my sweaty upper lip, I fell in love a little. Knowing there were hundreds of eyes on me and I was going to control how they felt for the next ninety minutes made me feel powerful. People had spent their hard-earned money on me and I didn't take that lightly. I had a responsibility to make them laugh.

Being onstage was sensational. It freaked me out how comfortable I was and how all my fear and self-doubt disappeared the second I heard the audience chanting my name. It was intoxicating, being adored like that. I felt high on all the adoration. At the end, I remember taking a bow and seeing everyone stand and cheer, and in that moment all I could think about was Brittany Murphy. I know it sounds so weird, but the adrenaline of being onstage was addictive. I totally understood how people could get addicted to fame and how their lives got completely turned upside down because of it. It is, in fact, addictive.

I bowed a few more times, leapt offstage, and proceeded to bang my knee into a speaker. I could've collapsed right there. I had never experienced something so painful in my life. I was blinded by the pain. I couldn't move. Nobody saw the bang, but they did see me hunched over looking constipated. I limped my way back to my dressing room, saw my family, and just cried. I wasn't sure if I was crying because I was overwhelmed by the emotion that comes from performing or because of the fact that I had probably caused permanent damage to my knee.

The next day, my second show at Carolines was just as epic. Except I was getting better. My timing was better, my jokes were better, the crowd was louder. Normal comedians get their start at five-minute open mics in front of an audience of a few people. They make their mistakes in clubs where the crowd doesn't give a shit about them. But I was practicing stand-up in front of sold-out crowds of people who knew me already. I was doing every-thing backward, which was a very on-brand thing for me to do.

After the second show, I found out that Ansel Elgort and Nicky Hilton were both in the crowd, along with some buyers and a few swanky agents from LA. They all came backstage to say hi after the show. I didn't think twice before giving Nicky Hilton a hug while wearing my pajamas from Amazon that were still damp with sweat. We all went out for drinks at the Boom Boom Room after the show, where I proceeded to black out—and this time it *was* tequila. I don't remember much about the night, but I do remember Ansel Elgort somehow got a ham-burger delivered to the middle of the club.

I felt like it was all really happening for me. I knew that this was going to be the start of something really different and special for me. I was no longer failing and I was really proud of myself. Stand-up is hard and I had done it. Not a lot of people can say that, but I could. I was ready to slay the third show at Carolines.

The third show never happened. That's because the show was scheduled to be on March 1, 2018, and we all know what ended up happening on February 28, 2018. Your girl got cancelled. I ended up cancelling the show for many reasons, one of them being I was so afraid of someone attacking me, verbally or otherwise. Another one of them being I couldn't physically get off my couch and stop crying long enough to put on a ninety-minute comedy show. I just wasn't feeling very funny.

A few months after the cancellation, on May 10, I made the very difficult decision to get back onstage. To be frank, it was the last thing I wanted to do. But Verizon had cancelled *The Morning Breath*, not a single brand was willing to touch me with a ten-foot pole, and *The Morning Toast* was just getting off the ground. I knew that doing this show was my only way back to myself and my fans, and to rebuilding the career I'd nearly lost. I had to put myself out there and take the risk. I didn't feel ready, but I didn't know if I would ever feel ready. When I look back on the last eight years of my career, I consider May 10, 2018, to be one of the most pivotal days of my life. I'm not entirely sure where I would be right now if I hadn't gotten back out there. I still can't believe that those shows sold out, even after all the drama of the cancellation. I also can't believe that I actually did them. Because it was a really brave thing to do and I don't think I could do it again.

I was more terrified for this show than I'd ever been. Carolines was gracious enough to let me come back, even though I was returning as a different person. I was now "controversial." I was nervous and *paranoid*. I had arranged for extra security because I was terrified someone might bring in a gun or something. I had a good friend, who works in media, give me a heads-up that there might be a group of protestors gathered outside of Carolines. I couldn't believe that this was my life now. How had I become this person? I was devastated but I didn't have time to give a shit. People were waiting for me and I was so fucking grateful that they had even come. I wanted—no, I *needed* to give them the best fucking comedy show they'd ever seen in their goddamn lives. And I did.

Hearing people clap for me again gave me a renewed sense of self. I had spent the last ten weeks wallowing in self-doubt, and that roaring applause was the validation I needed to keep moving. I had seriously thought about quitting the business and reverting to life as a normal twenty-three-year-old, but after that night, I knew I had made the right choice.

No protestors ever bothered to show up. Maybe because it was raining. Or maybe because I had faded back into irrelevancy and nobody actually gave a shit about me. I was totally okay with the latter. I had seen the good, the bad, and the ugly of what it means to be "famous" and I wasn't sure I was cut out for any of it. I'd always thought I had thick skin and was made for this life, but it wasn't so cut-and-dry anymore. A big part of me wanted nothing to do with the ugliness. But a bigger part of me loved performing. So I said "fuck 'em" and I booked three more shows at Carolines.

People were loving the show, and I was loving the fact that they were loving it. I wanted to capitalize on the momentum, so I flew to Chicago to see if the material was still funny in the Midwest (spoiler alert: it was).

What ended up happening was six months of chasing my fans around the country. I would do a show in Chicago, see people tweeting at me to come to Nashville, and hop on a plane to Nashville. Wherever I was wanted was where I would go. There was no real structure or routing at first because it was all so new. I had no agent or manager telling me what to do. It was a hot mess, but I was having too much success to care.

I eventually sold out enough shows to get the attention of the comedy industry. I had new agents from ICM, and we rolled out the official Girl With No Job comedy tour. We called it the Dirty Jeans Tour as an homage to a viral video I had made about the fact that I never wash my jeans. It was the perfect blend of my digital career and my new career in comedy. For the next eighteen months I did eighty-nine shows, most of which sold out.

The show was a beautiful culmination of all the things that I love: comedy, music, and pop culture. Every show was different, but I went out every night and wanted to make people happy, whether that included singing Celine Dion or dancing to the *Law & Order: SVU* theme song. The show was constantly evolving because insane shit was happening to me on the road and I loved incorporating those stories into my set. When someone sitting in the first row of my Miami show threw up on themselves, that became a bit. When someone in Dallas went to the bathroom during the show and somehow came back without pants on, that became a bit.

Aside from performing, my favorite part about being a touring comedian was the rider. For those who don't know, a rider is a list of things that, contractually, must be in your dressing room upon your arrival. Some musicians and comedians have outrageous demands like exotic animals or expensive champagne. I personally used the rider as an excuse to load up on snacks. My rider included the following:

* 6 Diet Cokes
* 6 Red Bulls
* 6 bottled waters
* 6 limes, a knife, and a cutting board
* 1 bottle of Don Julio 1942
* 1 fruit plate
* 1 bag of Baked Lay's
* 1 bag of Baked Ruffles

★ 1 bag of pretzels

★ 1 bag of peanut butter M&M's

★ 1 order of chicken tenders

★ 1 order of French fries (with a side of ketchup)

★ 2 high-powered fans

★ 1 full-length skinny mirror (no exceptions)

That's right. Picture me backstage, feet up, hair blowing in the breeze of a high-powered fan, licking French fry grease off my fingers while cutting limes for my preshow tequila shot. I was living the high life.

I started to develop this weird preshow ritual where I'd basically just power pose and yell at myself in the mirror. I'd also take a moment to pray and talk to God, because all these good things were happening for me and I didn't want Him to think I was ungrateful. Part of me thought that the 2018 cancellation had happened because God was punishing me for not being grateful for what I had. I had never taken the time to stop and be grateful for all the amazing things in my life, and I wasn't going to make that mistake again.

The venues were getting bigger and bigger. I was barely doing comedy clubs anymore, strictly theaters. I was genuinely so grateful. It's one thing to be popular online, but it's a whole other thing to see your popularity personified in real life. Seeing and hearing crowds of strangers stand up and chant your name is an indescribable feeling. It's unbelievable, and I'll never take it for granted. Thanks, God. You're a real one.

Life on the road wasn't exactly what Kate Hudson made it seem like in *Almost Famous*. What that movie neglected to prepare me for was the loneliness. I struggled with all the time I was spending away from my family and my husband. In the beginning, I cried myself to sleep most nights. Something about going from a room of fifteen hundred screaming fans to a lonely hotel room made me feel so isolated and depressed. I wasn't used to spending so much time alone. I've never lived alone before. I'm just the type of person who really doesn't like being alone. Mostly because I've seen one too many episodes of *Law & Order: SVU*, and so I constantly felt like there was an ax murderer in the closet of my hotel room.

I hated the feeling of life's going on without me at home. I felt like I was missing out on everything. It may sound silly but part of me thought that everyone back home would somehow stop living and wait for me to come back. But they went on with their lives even though I wasn't around, and that was hard for me to see.

Even though I was having a lot of success on tour, I was reluctant to keep adding shows because I was having such a hard time being away from home. It wasn't until my younger sister, Margo, made the very selfless decision to join me on tour that I finally began to have fun. She was in her senior year of college at NYU and was only taking a few classes, so she spent her weekends with me out on the road. It was the most selfless thing anyone had ever done for me and it completely changed my life.

Tour was no longer work. It was *fun*. Because everything with Margo is fun. I was no longer spending my nights looking at pictures of my dog, pining for him. I was no longer crying to Ben on FaceTime and making him stay on the line until I fell asleep. I was out, enjoying and celebrating my success with Margo. When I look back on the tour as a whole, I look at it through this wondrous lens where every night was a party, and that's all thanks to Margo. That feeling of missing my family went away because I was with my family. She was sleeping right next to me. I can't imagine ever being there for someone in the way that Margo was there for me, but that's because I'm a piece of shit and she's not. But if she's reading this—and she better be—I want her to know how grateful I am that she gave up two years in her twenties to spend every weekend in Bumfuck, America, with her older sister.

We made everything fun, even when it wasn't. We played Taylor Swift on our two-hour car rides from Columbus to Cincinnati. We played cards in every airport in America. After every show, we refused to go to bed. I was sweaty and exhausted, but Margo made sure we took advantage of it all. After the show in Huntsville, Alabama, we went to the Cole Swindell concert, snuck backstage, and somehow ended up in his personal dressing room bathroom. On our day off in Vancouver, we went to a dispensary and then ate our weight in popcorn at the movies. We saw a drag show in Charlotte. Margo competed in a twerk-off at a bar in Houston. We went to a strip club–slash–dive bar in Atlanta. We danced our faces off at the Brothers Osborne concert in Detroit.

I couldn't believe how much fun I was having in cities I had pretty much written off as irrelevant. People who live in New York City generally think of every other city as a shithole. It's a pretentious mindset that comes with being a jaded New Yorker. Spending two years of my life on the road shocked my entire belief system. Imagine how confused I was when I landed in Minneapolis and it wasn't one big farm. They actually had traffic lights and high-rise buildings.

The tour opened my eyes, not only to how many fabulous cities there are in this country but also to how some of them are—dare I say?—better than New York. I found myself picturing what my life would be like if I lived in these cities, because I was having so much fun exploring the bars, restaurants, and nightlife after my shows. The bars weren't nearly as cramped as they are in New York and the people were way nicer.

Thanks to *The Simple Life*, I had some preconceived notions about what people were going to look like or dress like in certain parts of the country, but can I just say, I have some of the most beautiful and stylish followers! And their boyfriends and husbands were my favorite part. Every now and then, a fan would bring their significant other to a meet-and-greet, and I absolutely loved making them feel special. I think I flirted with almost every single one of them, but hey, life on the road can be lonely.

What started with three hundred people in a small New York comedy club ended with a sold-out three-thousand-person show at the Beacon Theatre. Yeah, you heard me. The Beacon motherfucking Theatre. Jerry Seinfeld performs there! He's a real comedian! And I guess I am, too, now.

When the tour wrapped in my hometown, all I could feel was gratitude. I had started this tour as a last-ditch effort to salvage my career and I was ending it in front of three thousand people—something I had never thought was possible. I want to kiss every person who came to see me, because they changed my life. The Dirty Jeans Tour changed everything for me. It taught me to dream big because you never know what life has in store for you. I got to record a comedy special. I am writing a book, for Christ's sake. None of that would've been possible without the love and support of people who were able to forgive me, look past all my bullshit, and just laugh. How cool is that?

Tickets available at www.GirlWithNoJob.com :)

CHAPTER TEN

Oppositional and Defiant

Girl With No Job has taken me on quite a ride. Who would have thought that my incessant need for attention and desire for popularity would lead me to the career and life of my dreams? Well, maybe my therapist when she was calling me oppositional and defiant all those years ago. While I may no longer get lost in fits of rage like I used to, I'm still creating equal amounts of drama as I navigate new territory as an Instagram superstar.

From rubbing elbows with Elon Musk in LA to serenading Leonardo DiCaprio on a boat in Mexico, Girl With No Job has given me some of the biggest adventures I could have imagined.

It all began in a tiny dorm room in Greenwich Village, with a mini fridge full of muffins and a desire to avoid getting a real job. It turns out not wanting an ordinary job can evolve into a media company, podcast, morning show, and thriving Instagram if you try hard enough.

As delightfully charmed as my journey may seem, it hasn't been without its punch-in-the-face doses of humility and ass-kicking moments of failure. But those challenges have forced me to reflect, to learn, and to improve. For a while, as a young, insecure teenager, I thought I had to be mean in order to be funny. I would say and do crazy things at the expense of others to make myself feel powerful. I thought that was the only way to get people to like me. Isn't that sad? It took a global cancellation for me to learn that being mean isn't necessarily funny. Sometimes, it's just mean.

I learned more about myself during my 2018 cancellation than at any other time in my life. Of course, I could literally die from the amount of remorse and humiliation I feel when I reflect on that time, but the experience opened my eyes to the error of my ways and it ultimately softened me as a person. I used to think that being sensitive was a weakness, and now I've learned it's the exact opposite. I don't think I would have learned the importance of empathy, humility, and openness to your own shortcomings if I hadn't been hit hard and publicly with the cancellation humility stick.

Adversity is a necessary part of growth and until you realize that, you're not really ever going to evolve. As much as I would like to say I wish my dad had never died and I wish I had never gotten cancelled, these major life moments made me who I am. As difficult and soul shattering as they were, they rebuilt me stronger and smarter into the person that I was meant to be. You're not your worst moment, you're not your biggest mistake. What makes you who you are is how you handle those moments and mistakes.

When I look back on my career thus far, I feel an overwhelming sense of pride. I also feel a lot of shame, which I think is okay, too. If I didn't make it clear in the first nine chapters of this book, I am far from perfect.

I used to be very rigid, very hard-line, as if one fuckup should define a person. But after I went through the experience of being falsely labeled as so many things that I'm not and feeling so misunderstood, I finally understood that everything is not so black and white. I am now genuinely open to hearing what people have to say, even if it makes me uncomfortable. I acknowledge that there are two sides—or more!—to every story. My perception of the world can be so different from someone else's.

That's what makes Instagram so interesting. Through people's curated views of their lives, we see a different viewpoint of the world and a different set of experiences. It gives us a lens into other people's worlds, but it doesn't necessarily give us the full picture, of course. People show us what they want to show us, and what they don't show us is none of our fucking business.

The truth is that you just never know what someone's going through, or to use a cliché, you never know what happens behind closed doors. Most people who document their lives online only show part of who they are. It's not the whole picture. If followers remembered that they don't know the whole story of what people are going through, I think the culture of Instagram and social media would be a much more forgiving place.

People are too quick to jump all over someone or something without really considering the circumstances. We're all deserving of the opportunity to grow and the grace of second chances.

It's easy to forget the impact of your words, especially online, where the human connection is removed. My words have meaning, and when you talk as much as I do, it's easy to forget that. Unfortunately, you don't know the true impact of your words until you say something wrong. So how do we move forward in building healthier, more supportive and positive online communities? How do we continue to give fans and followers more details and revealing insights without opening ourselves up to unnecessary criticism?

I don't know if I have an answer. It starts with remembering that we're all learning and growing, and no one is perfect. Even if they post perfect pictures, with the perfect body and perfect clothes in their perfect house, they're human, with flaws and insecurities, an ex who won't call them back, a friend who disappointed them, a life dream that seems just out of reach. So let's stop holding everyone and everything on the Internet to an impossible standard.

I understand that the people who criticize you online feel, in their soul, that they're genuinely doing the right thing in calling you out. I know that there are people who hate me because they really think that I'm ignorant and racist. I acknowledge that because I have made my fair share of mistakes. Those mistakes shouldn't define me, yet they do. That's devastating to me, because at the end of the day, I like to think that generally I'm a good person. I mean well. Of course, I fuck up. That's why I love my Toast community so much: they continue to stand by me when I need them most. They allow me the grace to stumble and fall, to learn the lessons, and to be better.

I never want to exist in an echo chamber. Although I occasionally have unrealistic perceptions of my own fame and importance, I make a concerted effort to listen to the haters, to their opinions and critiques, because every now and then I actually learn something from them. It's important to know what you're doing wrong or what areas you need to improve in. But the Internet's not always a place that lends itself to giving you positive and helpful feedback.

When there's so much hate, the noise can get loud, and *that's* what keeps me up at night. I start to spiral, thinking maybe I am this terrible person. If enough people say you're dead, roll over, right?

When you put your head on your pillow at night, all you're left with is who you are. Can you live with yourself and the choices you make? I always keep the opinions of others in mind, but I refuse to let those voices guide me.

The thing is, if I didn't live a public life, I don't know that I would be pushing myself to be a better, different, more mature person. Without the accountability, I might just be complacent. The criticism and the critiques—and sometimes the rightful calling out—push me to examine myself and to hold myself to a higher standard.

Social media can be notoriously toxic, but it's important to remember that there is also so much positivity that comes from it—the community that it creates, the connections among people.

At the end of the day, all that really matters is my connection with my fans. Everything that I've been able to do is because of my fans, and I very much acknowledge that. If they're upset with me, that upsets me. I never ignore people's gripes with me as long as they're expressing them respectfully. I've tried to model my whole brand after Taylor Swift. People say the worst things about her, but ultimately, all she really cares about is her fans. So if somebody has something nasty to say about me, and they don't even like me, that bothers me less. What really bothers me is when a real fan of mine is upset, because they're the reason that all of this is happening for me.

I am the luckiest person in the world because of the Toasters. I'm so shook by the depth of the connection that fans feel when I see them on tour. In every city and town I visited, there were hordes of Toasters ready to embrace me, get drunk, and sing Celine Dion with me. It is an indescribable feeling to have someone that you've never met be so excited to meet you. I know the power of the fan connection because I feel that way about other people. The fact that people feel that way about me is so special and not something I take for granted.

When your career starts and mostly exists online, those moments of IRL connection are few and far between, and you hang on to them for as long as you can. I will literally replay my shows at the Beacon Theatre in my mind until the day I die. That feeling and that energy when the lights dimmed and the theater was packed with three thousand people screaming along to a Lizzo song in unison was electric. It was pure magic. There's power in recognizing yourself in the stories of the people that you follow or in the camaraderie of shared experiences and passions. On those nights, packed into theaters across the country, we were unstoppable. Long live, bitches.

Going through a controversy means the people who stand by you are *real* fans and really support you. It strengthens the bond.

The beginning of the Dirty Jeans Tour was right after my cancellation, and to see the fans come out for a night together in spite of all that had happened made us closer than ever. You never realize how big your platform is or how impactful your voice is until you really see that kind of reaction and see your fans stand by you.

I'm looking forward to growing with the Toast community, too. I love that we're sharing life's big milestones together and continuing to evolve. Digital influencers and Instagram communities can have real longevity, so when I think of the next five or ten years, I think of growing up with my followers. Just like when I got engaged and I was planning a wedding, I'll continue to document my personal life with millions of other people who are going through the same thing. When we start a family and I become a mom, I hope to do the same. I hope we can all grow up together while keeping it fresh. I just hope that Girl With No Job continues to be a real reflection of where I am in my life and that people can connect with that on any level. Girl With No Job will continue to grow up just as I do. I promise not to post about going to Coachella in a crochet bikini when I'm fifty, okay?

To say that I am living my dream life would be an understatement. When I was a kid, I rejected authority, and I wanted to be in charge of my life so badly. I wanted an apartment of my own and a boyfriend, and I didn't want to follow any rules. I grew up in a strict house and I hated it, so I couldn't wait to just be in charge of my own life. Now sometimes before I go to bed,

I think, *My fourteen-year-old self would be so proud of me*. I've got the nice apartment, I have a cute husband, and I'm kind of famous. The things that were important to me as a teenager, I made happen as an adult. I made my younger self proud! What more could I ask for?

When I walked onstage at the Beacon Theatre and heard three thousand people chanting my name, it occurred to me just how far I have come. When I was younger, I was called oppositional and defiant, told to channel my energy and to learn to express it. Well, standing onstage in silk pajamas, looking out at the faces of thousands of young men and women singing— no, belting—my song, I realized that I had finally learned the art of expression.

I am still proudly oppositional and defiant. I probably always will be. You should be, too. Never forget that you can forge your own path and use your own voice in whatever way you want. You don't have to play by the rules. RuPaul said it best: "The key to navigating this life—don't take it too seriously. That's when the party begins."

Let's resist the mundane and the boring. Let's defy authority! I wish for you all the kind of unusual, outrageous, and challenging journey that I've had. Take it from this disgraced queen, it's a much more interesting way to go through life.

A toast to the wild ones!